HEIDEGGER ON KANT'S First *Critique* and Other Essays

R.K. Gupta

APPLE BOOKS

Heidegger on Kant's First *Critique* and Other Essays

First Edition 2011

Published by

APPLE BOOKS
1/9929, 1st Floor, West Gorakh Park,
Gali No. 3-H, Shahdara, Delhi 110032
Tel.: 9810429755, 8800794724
E-mail: alankar_books07@yahoo.com

ISBN 978-81-920778-1-9

Distributed by
K.K. PUBLICATIONS
4806/24, Bharat Ram Road
Darya Ganj, New Delhi 110002
Tel.: 23285079, 23285167
E-mail: kkpdevinder@vsnl.net

Layout by Ritesh Kumar

Typeset at JMD Publisher Services, New Delhi 110044

Printed in India *by* Rajesh Tandon for Apple Books

Contents

Preface

All the articles contained in this volume have already been published as follows:

1. 'A Difficulty in Kant's *Critique of Pure Reason* and Heidegger's Kant-Interpretation,' published in German under the title, 'Eine Schwierigkeit in Kants *Kritik der reinen Vernunft* und Heideggers Kant-Interpretation,' *Zeitschrift für philosophische Forschung*, Vol. VI, No. 3, 1962.
2. Wittgensteins's Theory of 'Family Resemblances' in his *Philosophical Investigations* (Sections 65–80)', *Philosophie Naturalis*, Vol. 12, No. 3, 1970.
3. 'Kant's Definition of an Analytic Proposition', *International Studies in Philosophy*, Vol. VIII, 1976.
4. 'What is a Criterion? Some Reflections', *Philosophie Naturalis*, Vol. 17, No. 2, 1978.
5. 'Kant's Definition of an Analytic Proposition—A Further Consideration', *Akten des 5 Internationalen Kant-Kongresses*, 1981, Bouvier Verlag Bonn.
6. 'Reasons in Ethics', *Universitas*, Vol. 25, No. 2, 1981.
7. 'Analytic and Synthetic Propositions', *Archiv für Geschichte der Philosophie*, Vol. 64, No. 1, 1982.
8. 'Phenomenalism, Idealism and Mentalism' *Philosophie Naturalis*, Vol. 21, No. 1, 1984.
9. 'Public and Private Use of Reason', *Gandhi Marg*, July–September 1995.
10. 'Morality of Means', *Gandhi Marg*, April–June, 1996.

11. Kant's Doctrine of Categories: An Attempt at Some Clarification', *Journal of Indian Council of Philosophical Research*, Vol. XIV, No. 1, 1996.
12. Knowledge and Morality', *Gandhi Marg*, April–June, 1997.
13. 'Notes on Kant's Derivation of the Various Formulae of the Categorical Imperative', *International Journal of Philosophical Studies*, Vol. 5, No. 3, 1997.
14. 'Telling a Lie', *Journal of Indian Council of Philosophical Research*, Vol. XV, No. 1 September–December 1997.
15. 'Putting into Practice What One Professes', *Journal of Indian Council of Philosophical Research*, Vol. XV, No. 3, May–August 1998.
16. 'Moral Exceptions', *Journal of Indian Council of Philosophical Research*, Vol. XVII, No. 1, 2001.

I am grateful to the editors of the journals concerned for kindly publishing them. These articles are of two kinds: firstly, there are those which are historical-critical in nature. They mainly concern Kant's philosophy. Secondly, there are those which deal with some or the other problem, about which I have found myself worrying. They are moral in nature, and are concerned with such problems as these: what is the extent of a person's obligation to a body of which he is a member? Should society lay down any limits whatsoever to academic debate? What are the moral qualities which a person needs to have in his pursuit of knowledge? Do not all means have a moral character to the extent they are productive of a moral end? What are the conditions under which not following a moral law may be morally in order? What role or roles does the notion of telling a lie play in our life, besides the moral one? Several of the articles have been discussed in the weekly meetings of St. Stephen's College Philosophy Society. I am grateful to its members for their comments.

Delhi R.K. Gupta

1

A Difficulty in Kant's *Critique of Pure Reason* and Heidegger's Kant-Interpretation

MY AIM IN this paper is to bring to light a certain difficulty in Kant's attempt to show the possibility of synthetic *a priori* propositions in his *Critique of Pure Reason*.[1] In this respect I propose to consider Heidegger's attempt to solve this difficulty in his *Kant und das Problem der Metaphysik*.[2] I also propose to mention at some length the further interpretation which Heidegger places upon his solution. I may point out here that in doing all this I am not presupposing that there are synthetic *a priori* propositions. Perhaps there are not.[3] I am mainly contending that at least as regards Kant's attempt to found them, there is a certain difficulty, and that Heidegger's attempt to solve this difficulty, though having much to say for itself in its own right, is unwarranted as it is and looks like begging the question at issue.

The paper is divided into three parts. In the first part, after stating the problem of synthetic *a priori* propositions as such, I will state Kant's attempt to show the possibility of these propositions, and then point out the difficulty with regard to his attempt. In the second part, I will firstly explain Heidegger's attempt to solve this difficulty, and secondly mention the further interpretation which he places on his solution. Finally, in the third part, I will give in all two criticisms of Heidegger's attempt, and, without an examination as to the plausibility of his further interpretation of his solution, I will give a greater statement about its nature.

1. (a) The problem of synthetic *a priori* propositions

We all know today that Hume divided propositions into two kinds, concerning, firstly, 'matters of fact', and secondly, 'relations of ideas', and contended that neither of them provided us with any knowledge.

As far as the propositions of the former kind are concerned, Hume thought that they were purely empirical. That is to say, they depended solely upon experience, and on nothing else whatsoever. For example, a proposition like 'Fire burns the hand' or 'All Indians are sentimental' are propositions of this kind. Either of them makes an assertion about something on the basis of facts given in experience. There is absolutely no other way in which they are possible. Kant called such propositions synthetic *a posteriori*.

Hume thought that any proposition, which depended solely upon experience in the above sense never has a logical basis, that is, it is never absolutely certain, or universal and necessary. When we say 'Fire burns the hand' or 'All Indians are sentimental', then we say so merely on the basis of our past experience of those cases when fire has been found to burn the hand or Indians have been found to be sentimental, respectively. This past experience, generally in proportion to its abundance, produces in us an expectation, gives birth to a habit to expect, that what has been found to happen in the past will probably repeat itself in the future also. There is no doubt that if the evidence of our past experience has been extremely abundant, then our expectation would considerably increase, nay, even reach very near certainty, as in the case of fire burning the hand, but it would never reach complete certainty. For one may still doubt whether what has been found to happen in the past, however exhorbitant the evidence for it, would actually repeat itself in the future. It follows, therefore, that all propositions regarding matters of fact are always psychologically based and thus are contingent. They never constitute knowledge proper, that is, knowledge which is absolutely certain, or universal and necessary. I think that it must be admitted with Hume that experience alone can never give us knowledge. In other words, pure empiricism leads necessarily to complete scepticism with regard to knowledge. It is pure psychologism.

Further, as far as propositions of the latter kind, i.e., those concerning relations of ideas, are concerned, Hume thought that they were purely analytic. That is, negatively speaking, they had nothing whatsoever to do with experience in the way of dependence and, positively speaking, they involved in the predicate term a mere analysis of the subject term. For example, a proposition like 'A is A' or 'A triangle is a three-angled figure' are propositions of this kind. In neither of them is an assertion made about a matter of fact given in experience. Each is a mere analysis in the predicate term of what is already there in the subject term. Kant called such propositions analytic *a priori*.

Hume thought that any proposition, which does not depend upon experience but involves in the predicate term a mere analysis of the subject term, is purely logical or mathematical. When we say 'A is A' or 'A triangle is a three-angled figure', then we do not say anything which in any way depends upon experience and is thus contingent, but merely make explicit in the predicate term what is already implicit in the subject term. It is quite clear that in any such case we are saying something which is absolutely certain, or universal and necessary. However much we may try to alter its truth, we can never succeed in doing go.

Now, true as it is, no propositions concerning relations of ideas ever constitute knowledge. For, as Hume contended, knowledge implies, besides the characteristics of universality and necessity, that we say in the predicate term something over and above what has already been said in the subject term. In this way only empirical or synthetic *a posteriori* propositions can, if at all, constitute knowledge. For in them alone do we say something in the predicate term which is not already there in the subject term, but is first obtained through experience and then added to it. Purely analytic propositions never say anything in the predicate term over and above what is already there in the subject term. In other words, they are merely identical or tautologous propositions.

What is it that follows from the above considerations? It follows: negatively, that knowledge cannot be possible in terms of propositions of either the former or the latter kind. The former lead to complete scepticism or psychologism, and the latter give us mere identical or tautologous propositions; positively, that knowledge can be possible only when we have propositions which resemble, firstly, propositions of the former kind, insofar as they say in the predicate term something which is over and above what has already been said in the subject term, without being for that reason empirical or *a posteriori;* and secondly, that they resemble those of the latter kind, insofar as they are universal and necessary or *a priori,* without being for that reason analytic. That is to say, knowledge can be possible only when we have propositions, which are, on the one hand, what we may call synthetic, and on the other hand, *a priori.*

Now, Hume did not think that there were propositions which had both these characteristics. Therefore, he did not admit that there was any knowledge.

(b) Kant's attempt to show their possibility

It must be recognized in the very beginning that if synthetic *a priori* propositions are to be possible, then they must not have anything to do with either synthetic *a posteriori* or analytic *a priori* propositions. That is to say, in the first instance, they must not be empirical in the sense of being derived from experience. If that were so, then as I have shown above, they would be merely contingent and thus would not constitute knowledge. In the second instance, they must not be analytic in the sense of making explicit in the predicate term what is already implicit in the subject term. If that were so, then they would be merely identical or tautologous, i.e., would not say in the predicate term anything over and above what has already been said in the subject term, and thus again would not constitute knowledge.

In other words, if synthetic *a priori* propositions are to be possible, then they must be of a peculiar sort, resembling, as I have said: synthetic *a posteriori* propositions only insofar as they assert in the predicate term something over and above what is already asserted in the subject term; and analytic *a priori* propositions only insofar as they are universal and necessary or *a priori*. Otherwise they must be absolutely different from either of them.

The question arises: if synthetic *a priori* propositions have nothing to do with or are absolutely different from either of the other two sets of propositions, then, how are they possible? Where do we find them? In what way are they justified? We have seen above how propositions of either of the two other types are possible: we derive one from experience; and we obtain the other from the analysis of the subject term in the predicate term. With regard to either of them there is no problem. The problem arises with regard to the propositions which are neither of them but which resembled the former in being synthetic and the latter in being *a prori*. Question is: how are we to obtain such propositions? Where are they to be found? What is to account for their possibility?

The notion of synthetic *a priori* propositions implies that they are: firstly, synthetic. That is, they relate themselves in the predicate term to something, some object which is not a part of the subject term; secondly, they are *a priori*. That is, they so relate themselves in a universal and necessary manner. This means to say that the notion of synthetic *a priori* propositions implies that there are certain universal and necessary ways or manners in which we can relate ourselves to objects. The question is: are there such ways or manners? And if so, how or where are they to be found?

Now, it is quite obvious that if there are such ways or manners, they cannot be found in the nature of an object to which we relate ourselves in the predicate term universally and necessarily. For, as I have pointed out above, objects, that is, the experience of objects gives us only synthetic *a posteriori* propositions, i.e., ways or manners in which we can relate ourselves to objects in the predicate term only contingently. Hence if we have to discover such ways or manners as we require, then they must be searched for, not in the nature of objects, but, if at all, in our own nature, i.e. in the nature of the subject itself. The question is; are there any ways or manners in our own selves in which, we can relate ourselves in the predicate term to objects universally and necessarily? And if there are, what are they?[4]

Now, Kant thought that there were such ways or manners in our own self, which accounted for the possibility of synthetic *a priori* propositions. It is needless to say that the whole of his *Critique of Pure Reason* is a discussion of this problem. Presently I shall explain in short his consideration of it there.

According to Kant, there are two ways or manners, or what he calls faculties, in ourself i.e. in mind, which account for the possibility of synthetic *a priori* propositions or knowledge. The first he calls the faculty of sensibility, and the other that of understanding. As far as the former faculty is concerned, its function is solely to receive an object. This means to say that whenever we receive an object it must be through or by means of sensibility, and in no other way whatsoever. Thus, according to Kant, the mind's capacity to receive an object and sensibility are identical terms. There is absolutely no difference between the two.[5]

Kant maintains that whenever sensibility receives an object, which it must in order to be there at all, it does so in either of the two forms: firstly, in the form of space, and secondly, in that of time. Here it may be asked: what does Kant mean by space? What does he mean by time? And how does he consider them to be forms of sensibility?

Now, Kant supposes that space is the way in which mind or sensibility receives an object as outside us. That is to say, whenever we receive an object as arranged in what are called spatial relations, for instance, the relations of side by side, above, behind and so on, then we can be said to receive it in space, or, which is the same thing as saying, in the form of space. For this reason Kant also calls space the outer sense. Thus, for him, space, the outer sense, the mind's or sensibility's capacity to receive objects in the relations of side by side and so on, are identical terms.

Further, Kant supposes that time is the way in which mind or sensibility receives an object as inside us. That is to say, whenever we receive an object as arranged in what is called temporal relation, namely the relation of before and after, then we can be said to receive it in time, or, which is the same thing as saying, in the form of time. For this reason Kant also calls time the inner sense. Thus, for him, time, the inner sense, the mind's or sensibility's capacity to receive objects in the relation of before and after, are identical terms.

However, insofar as even the objects of outer sense must ultimately be received by or belong to inner sense, time can be said to be the way in which the mind or sensibility receives any object whatsoever, as outside or inside us. We may merely say that it, i.e. time, receives an outer object mediately and an inner object immediately. But at any rate it must receive *all* objects.

As far as the latter faculty, namely the faculty of understanding, is concerned, its function is not, like that of sensibility, to receive an object. That is to say, an object could be received without the understanding being there: in this sense an object is independent of understanding. Its function, on the other hand, is to operate upon an object which has been received by sensibility. Thus it is in terms of this operation alone that an object depends upon understanding. It is interesting to note here that, according to Kant, not only can an object, as received, exist, without understanding, but understanding can also exist without its function of operation upon the object in question.[6]

It is only when we want to obtain synthetic *a priori* propositions that the latter must assume its above-mentioned function with regard to the former.

Kant maintains that whenever understanding operates upon an object of sensibility, which it must do in order to make synthetic *a priori* propositions possible, it does so in terms of several of its concepts or categories.[7]

Now, I do not intend to mention here these concepts or make any comments on them. As a matter of fact, my purpose at present is not to show that there are synthetic *a priori* propositions, and if there are what they are and how they are possible,—whether they are possible in terms of the mind's faculties of sensibility and understanding or something else; nor is it to show whether Kant's own description of the two faculties in question is justified, and if not, what is their correct description. My task at present is none of these. On the contrary, it is merely to logically follow Kant's attempt to found synthetic *a priori* propositions, and to point out a certain difficulty which I face with regard to it.

I would be satisfied here by merely pointing out that what has above been called the operation of understanding *upon* the object as received by means of sensibility is the activity of unification or synthesis. Kant supposes that an object as it is received by sensibility is a disorderly manifold; it has no unity whatsoever yet. It comes to have unity only when the mind comes to operate upon it by means of what have above been called concepts of understanding. These concepts are the mind's own ways of unifying or synthesizing the object of sensibility which is received only as a disorderly manifold. Without them an object of sensibility would remain disorderly. Kant says that 'intuitions without concepts are blind', meaning by the former the object of sensibility. But he also says that 'concepts without intuitions are empty', meaning thereby that if the former have to have any meaning, then they must be related or must apply to the latter. Any concept for Kant has meaning only if it applies to or has relation with intuitions, i.e. functions as one of the conditions of the possibility of synthetic *a priori* propositions, i.e. knowledge. Otherwise, though it does continue to exist, it is empty.

Now, according to Kant, synthetic *a priori* propositions become possible, because the mind has the capacity, firstly, to receive an object, not this or that object but any object whatsoever (object in general = x), and secondly, to operate upon the object so received in the way of unification or synthesis. By the combination of the two faculties of sensibility and understanding we obtain a set of propositions, which, on the one hand, are not derived from objects of experience and thus are not empirical or synthetic *a posteriori* and on the other hand, do not express mere identical or tautologous propositions; but which are (i) synthetic, insofar as they apply or relate themselves to an object which is not contained in the subject, and (ii) *a priori,* insofar as they express universal and necessary ways in which subject and object are related with each other. Kant mentions a number of such propositions in the chapter 'Analytic of Principles' of his *Critique of Pure Reason.* It is not necessary for me here to mention and explain them in any way.

(c) Difficulty with regard to Kant's attempt

Here it would be clear that we are in the midst of a certain difficulty and with regard to this Kant gives a certain solution also. The difficulty is this. It is easy to see how sensibility is related to an object. Sensibility, as we have seen, is the faculty or capacity of the mind to receive an object, in such a manner that it is what it is in receiving an object : it has no other being apart from this fact of receiving. Similarly, an object also, in the sense in which we can at all talk of it, must be received by sensibility. This means to say that both sensibility and its object are *essentially* interrelated. We cannot think of the one without the other. I have pointed out above that we can express this fact by saying that sensibility is object-related (similarly we may also say that object is sensibility-related) or that, in the words of

Heidegger, it is of the nature of transcendence. Neither exists by itself, i.e. in isolation from the other.

However, it is not easy to see how understanding is related to an object. Understanding, as we have seen, is the faculty or capacity of the mind to operate upon (i.e. unify or synthesize) an object as received by sensibility; it does not itself receive, or even create an object.[8] This means to say that an object is there, as received, without understanding. Not only that. As I have said above understanding also exists, though in an empty manner, without the object of sensibility, i.e. without any object whatsoever. It follows that between understanding and its object there is not the same sort of essential relationship as there is between sensibility and its object. And therefore, the question may be asked: how does understanding relate itself to its object? If there is not the same sort of relationship between understanding and its object as there is between sensibility and its object, then, is there no essential relationship between them? If there is, then how? If there is not, then what makes their relationship possible?

Now, as far as the question about the nature of the relationship between understanding and its object is concerned, Kant maintains that it is essential, not because the latter would not just be without the former, but because it would not be unified or synthesized, i.e. known, without it We have seen above that an object as received by sensibility is a disorderly manifold; it does not have any unity whatsoever yet. In order for it to become an object of knowledge, i.e. of synthetic *a priori* propositions, it must be brought to unity. And this is possible, as we have seen, only in terms of the operations of understanding. Otherwise not.

So far it seems to be clear. That is, it is clear that, in order to become an object of knowledge, a disorderly manifold of sensibility must be unified or synthesized. For how else would it be possible as an object of knowledge? The difficulty arises when we raise the question about the possibility of unification or synthesis of the object of knowledge itself. For the question now is: how does understanding, which has nothing whatsoever to do with its object in the same essential way as sensibility has to do with its, yet relate itself to it? How does it do so? We grant that it does so in the way of unification or synthesis. But how does such a unification or synthesis itself take place? By what means?

We may put our question differently also. We have seen that as far as sensibility is concerned, it is related to its object in an essential manner, i.e. in a manner that neither of them would just be without the other. In this connection I have chosen to say, in accordance with Heidegger's terminology, that sensibility is of the nature of transcendence. There is little doubt that it is in this sense that it can function as a condition of the possibility of synthetic a *priori* propositions. However, as far as understanding is concerned, it is not related to its object in the same essential manner, and therefore cannot be said to be of the nature of transcendence. There is no doubt that it does relate itself to its object in the way of unification or synthesis. But the question is; how does it do so? What makes its application to the object of sensibility possible so that we may say that understanding, like sensibility, is also of the nature of transcendence, and thus in a position to function as the other condition of the possibility of synthetic *a priori* propositions? It is obvious that unless we can do so, our hope of justifying the propositions in question must come to naught.

Kant tries to solve this difficulty in terms of what he calls transcendental imagination. He supposes that "by its means we bring the manifold of intuitions (i.e. object of sensibility) on the one hand, into connection with the condition of the necessary unity of pure apperception (i.e. understanding)[10] on the other. The two extremes, namely sensibility and understanding, must stand in a necessary connection with each other through the mediation of this transcendental function of imagination . . .".[11]

Now, with regard to this statement of Kant, the following questions arise. Firstly, what does he mean by transcendental imagination itself? Does he mean to say that there is, besides sensibility and understanding which he has already mentioned, a third faculty also which is involved in knowledge and the function of which is to unite or synthesize the other two? If so, what does he mean by saying, as we all know that he does, that there are two and only two faculties involved in all knowledge, namely those of sensibility and understanding? If not, what else does he mean?

Secondly, how does transcendental imagination, supposing that there is something like that, perform its function? That is to say, how is it possible for it to mediate between two completely divergent faculties of sensibility and understanding? Must it not, in order to do so, firstly, partake of the nature of one, and then of the other? But how can it do so without at the same time being either of them? And if that is so, must it not imply that all the faculties are ultimately identical each with a dual purpose? There is no doubt that if the notion of synthetic *a priori* proposition or transcendence is to form a unity, which it must and which Kant undoubtedly wants it to do, then any number of elements involved in it can be considered only as its aspects or moments, and not discrete parts combined together in an external or arbitrary manner.

Again, in connection with our very problem of the relationship between sensibility and understanding, on page 197 of the *Critique of Pure Reason*, Kant points out that ". . . there must be some third thing, which is homogeneous on the one hand with the category (of understanding)[12] and on the other hand with the appearance (of sensibility)[12] and which thus makes the application of the former to the latter possible. This mediating representation must be pure, that is, void of all empirical content, and yet at the same time, while it must in one respect be *intellectual*, it must in another be *sensible*. Such a representation is the *transcendental schema*." This transcendental schema is time or a certain transcendental determination of time, which, according to him, "is so far homogeneous with the category, which constitutes its unity, in that it is universal and rests upon an *a priori* rule. But, on the other hand, it is so far homogeneous with appearance, in that time is contained in every empirical (sensible)[13] representation of the manifold."[14]

Here it would be immediately asked: what is the transcendental schema or determination of time? We have seen before that the function of time is to receive an object. If that is so, in what relationship does this function of time stand to what is here called its schema or determination? And, then, time being what it has been supposed to be, how can a determination of it ever be intellectual or homogeneous with the category?

Moreover, what is the relationship between transcendental imagination and the transcendental schema or determination of time? As mediators between sensibility and understanding are the two identical? If so, how?

It is clear that the answer to the first question should be possible in the light of the answer to the second. For if we could once find out that there was an intrinsic or essential relation between the two mediators in question, then it would be easy to determine what role time played, besides that of receiving an object, that is to say, whether it was intellectual as well as sensible, or what was really meant by the transcendental schema or determination of time.

Now, as regards the second question, Kant points out that the schema "is a product and, as it were, a monogram, of pure (transcendental) *a priori* imagination."[15] This means to say that the transcendental imagination produces or makes possible the transcendental schema or determination of time. Kant compares the schema with the image in psychology, with the difference that the former is a pure, and not an empirical image. Insofar as, according to Kant, transcendental imagination has to do with both sensibility and understanding, we may say that it determines or rather cuts out images in the manifold of time (i.e. intuitions) in accordance with the categorial unities of understanding (i.e. concepts), in such a manner that a particular image or schema corresponds with a particular category. Kant mentions different schemas corresponding to his four classes of categories.[16]

Now, I do not understand in any clear terms what Kant really means by transcendental imagination,[17] and how he makes it play the role of a mediator between sensibility and understanding.[18] Does he mean to say—as I have pointed out above that he must do so in order to make it play this role—that it partakes of the nature of both sensibility and understanding in such a manner that all three of them are ultimately shown to be identical each with a dual purpose? If so, how does it happen? The question whether it produces the schema or determines time in the above-mentioned manner should obviously be said to depend upon our first knowing what it is and does, and may therefore be abandoned for our present purpose.

With regard to this difficulty, in the following part of the present paper, I intend to explain Heidegger's understanding of the nature of transcendental imagination so as to make it play its alleged role. I also intend to show how he interprets the nature of transcendental imagination in such a manner that it is found to be identical with what he calls the original notion of time (die ursprüngliche Zeit).

2. (a) Heidegger's understanding of the nature of transcendental imagination so as to make it play its alleged role

I have explained before that the problem of synthetic *a priori* propositions is with regard to the essential unity of subject and object. In this connection I have used Heidegger's expression to say that it is the problem of the nature of transcendence.[19]

This means to say that if sensibility and understanding, as conjoined by transcendental imagination, have to function as the bases of synthetic *a priori* propositions, then they all must form an essential unity. The question is how it is possible. Now, Heidegger thinks that both sensibility and understanding do form a unity, and that this is possible in terms of transcendental imagination itself. In the following part of this section I propose to explain how he shows this to be the case.

In the first instance, Heidegger does not suppose that transcendental imagination is some third faculty,[20] which functions as an external mediator between the other two faculties, though Kant often seems to give the impression that this is so.[21] If that were so, then, firstly, we would be faced with the same sort of difficulty as we were with regard to the relationship between sensibility and understanding. For it would be asked here: how can this external mediator mediate between two things with which it has nothing intrinsically to do? And secondly, it would be impossible to reconcile this view with Kant's own major view that there are two and not more than two sources of synthetic *a priori* propositions.

On the contrary, Heidegger supposes that transcendental imagination is the ground or root of both sensibility and understanding.[22] This means that it is not anything separate from them, but is that common source from which either of them derives its being or essential character.[23] I will explain here how, according to Heidegger, it is essentially related, on the one hand, to sensibility, and on the other, to understanding, and thus is in a position to play its alleged role.

(i) Transcendental imagination and sensibility

We have seen before that, for Kant, sensibility signifies mind's capacity to receive an object ultimately in the universal form of time. The question arises: what does it as such have to do with transcendental imagination?

According to Heidegger, sensibility is not merely passive insofar as it receives an object, but also active insofar as it forms (bildet)[24] the object in terms of its universal form. This means to say that it is not merely receptive as though everything came to it absolutely unformed or unshaped or unsynthesized: it is formative (bildende) also in such a way that anything that came to it is arranged in a certain manner. We may express this fact differently also by saying that, in receiving an object, sensibility forms it as well, in such a manner that receiving and forming are not its two different activities, but one and the same activity with what one may call its two distinct aspects or moments. This activity of sensibility Kant calls the synopsis of the manifold of intuitions. We may do well here to mention Kant's statement, which Heidegger quotes in his book from Kant's *Reflections:*[25] "Raum und Zeit sind die Formen der Vorbildung in der Anschauung."

Now, Heidegger supposes that the above-mentioned capacity of sensibility, which consists in forming an object in the very mode of its receiving it, is due to transcendental imagination. We know that the function of imagination, or rather productive imagination, is to form or combine or picture in its own manner an object given to it. Transcendental imagination, as distinguished from what we may call psychological imagination, does not of course deal with empirical objects so as to make anything out of them. It is purely *a priori* and deals with an object in general = x to do whatever with it. It is in this sense that Heidegger thinks that it has essentially to do with sensibility, or that the latter partakes of the nature of the former.

(ii) Transcendental imagination and understanding

From the above it becomes clear that in order to have an essential relationship with transcendental imagination, understanding must be formative in the same sense as sensibility. That is to say, it must have an object given to it which it would form. However, as we have seen before, there is no object whatsoever of which we would say that it is related in the same manner as sensibility. It has at its disposal a number of unities or concepts by means of which it could form an object: needless to say that the function of all these unities is formative. But it has no object which it could form. Thus the question arises: what is it that it forms? Or, how does it come to have an essential relationship with transcendental imagination?

Here Heidegger takes a certain step which looks like begging the question. He identifies understanding with schematism,[26] with the result that what have so far been considered concepts, existing independently and belonging to sensibility at any rate not essentially or ontologically, become mere schemata, i.e. formations or determinations of the manifold of intuitions by means of transcendental imagination. There should be no difficulty in seeing that if this is so, understanding does no more remain an independent faculty, which Kant thought it was and due to which reason one has had the problem of explaining the possibility of relationship between it and sensibility, but is dissolved into transcendental imagination itself.

It follows from the above consideration of the relationship between transcendental imagination, on the one hand, and sensibility and understanding, on the other, that the latter are not two independent faculties between which some sort of relationship would have to be shown for the possibility of synthetic *a priori* propositions. They, in fact, are or are grounded or rooted in one and the same faculty, the faculty of transcendental imagination, the purpose of which is two-fold: to receive an object, and, in the same process to form it.

(b) Transcendental imagination and time

I have shown above that, according to Kant, synthesis is not altogether foreign even to sensibility. I have said that he uses the word 'synopsis' to indicate that mode of synthesis which takes place at this level. In this sense we may agree with Heidegger to say that sensibility is formative. In all Kant enumerates and explains three different modes of synthesis which are necessary for the possibility of knowledge or synthetic *a priori* propositions.[27] They are the following:

1. The synthesis of Apprehension in Intuition.
2. The synthesis of Reproduction in Imagination.
3. The synthesis of Recognition in a Concept.

Now, insofar as transcendental imagination has been shown to be the ground or root of both sensibility and understanding, it must be admitted that these three modes belong to it only. This means to say that it synthesizes the manifold of intuitions in a three-fold manner, as, firstly, apprehension, then, reproduction and lastly, recognition. In this place I would like to quote the following lines from Heidegger. He states that the three-fold synthesis in question does not mean that "die Apprehension u.s.f. einer Synthesis unterworfen werden, auch nicht, dass die Apprehension bzw die Reproduction und Rekognition eine Synthesis vollziehen, sondern dass die Synthesis als solche den Character entweder der Apprehension oder der Reproduktion oder der Rekognition hat. Die Austrücke bedeuten demnach: Synthesis im Modus der Apprehension, Reproduktion und Rekognition oder: Synthesis als apprehendierende, als reproduzierende und als rekognisierende. Kant handelt also von der Synthesis, d. h. vom Vermögen der Synthesis im Hinblickauf diese drei Modi als die ihr in spezifische Weise eigentlichen".[28]

Before we come to deal with Heidegger's account to show how the above-mentioned three modes of synthesis refer in an essential manner to the three aspects of time, namely present, past and future, respectively, and thus together constitute what Heidegger calls original time, it may be asked: does it not appear from the above statement of the three modes of synthesis that transcendental imagination is only one of them, and by no means the ground or root of the other two? On page 161 of his book Heidegger asserts that it is so.[29] But on the same page, a little later, he also asserts that transcendental imagination is the root, and that this is so is confirmed by his interpretation of it in terms of time.[30] I must confess that I find the situation confusing, and gain no light from Heidegger himself with regard to the reconciliation of these two contradictory assertions.

I will devote the rest of the present section to explaining Heidegger's interpretation of the three modes of synthesis in terms of time.

Heidegger (and also Kant) supposes that for each of the three modes of pure synthesis, with which we are here primarily concerned, there is an empirical counterpart. That is to say, there is, firstly, an empirical synthesis of empirical apprehension, secondly, that of empirical reproduction and thirdly, of empirical recognition. Now, in all these modes we, in the first instance, refer ourselves to some or the other empirical object or objects, and, in the second instance, unite these objects by an essential reference to time. Now, as far as the former is concerned there is no difficulty. In all the modes in question we do refer ourselves to some or the other empirical objects. Difficulty arises with regard to the latter, i.e. how, in respect of them, synthesis is possible only *by* an essential reference to time. Heidegger explains it in the following manner.

In the manifold of objects, which, according to Kant, we receive in every intuition, we must be able to distinguish the time (i) of one object from that of another, i.e. the 'now' of one from that of another, and hold the 'nows' of all of them together; (ii) of that which has taken place before or at an earlier time, i.e., the 'now' of that which is no more, and hold it in reproduction (behalten können); and (iii) of that which can take place after or at a later time, i.e. not yet, and hold it forth for recognition (vorhalten können).[31] It is only in terms of this three-fold distinction of objects in time, which constitute present, past and future objects, respectively, that the three-fold synthesis in question is possible. Further, it should be clear that these three distinctions of objects in time, as referring to the three distinctions of one and the same synthesis must themselves belong to a unity. We must also say that in this unity the future object plays the leading or predominant role, for it is that which ultimately accounts for the character of self-sameness of an object (by means of recognition).

Now, as far as the three modes of pure synthesis, that of pure apprehension, that of pure reproduction and that of pure recognition, are concerned, it is clear that they do not refer to any empirical object whatsoever, but to what has been called above an object in general = ẋ. As I have shown, this object is one to which we are essentially related and, which we, i.e. our transcendental imagination, as the ultimate ground or root of all other synthesis, forms just as it receives.

Now, if the synthesis or unity of this object is to be possible by an essential reference to time, which we have seen to be the case with empirical synthesis and which Heidegger supposes is also the case here, then, it is clear that this object would be essentially related to time itself, i.e., would be that which time would form in the same process in which it receives it. In other words, time would be of the nature of transcendence. There is no doubt that this is also the meaning of Heidegger's attempt to identify transcendental imagination with his notion of original time. In the following part of the present section I will give a brief account of Heidegger's attempt to show how the synthesis or unity of an object in general is to be understood in terms of its essential reference to time, and how, as a result of this, transcendental imagination is seen to be identical with it. It will be found that his argument here is analogical to what we have seen to be the case with empirical synthesis.

In the absence of a manifold of empirical objects or intuitions, with regard to the empirical synthesis of which we distinguished time into its three-fold aspect, we have now a manifold of pure objects or intuitions. It has been shown that these objects or intuitions are those with regard to which we are of the nature of transcendence, i.e. which we form just as we receive them. Now, if we understand this transcendence as a unity, which we must from what has been said above, then, we may somewhat paradoxically say that this is a 'self-forming-self-receiving' unity (das hinnehmende Bilden). The question arises: what does the measure of 'now', which we have seen to distinguish one object or intuition of the empirical manifold from another and to hold all of them together in its three-fold aspect, refer to in the pure manifold? That is, what does it distinguish and hold together? In the first place, it is clear that it is time alone which can distinguish one object of the pure manifold from another by the distinction of different 'nows' in their three-fold aspect. In the second place, insofar as transcendence is a 'self-forming-self-receiving unity, the manifold of objects or intuitions can be nothing but the manifold of 'nows' giving itself unity in its three-fold aspect: as (i) holding together different 'nows' as distinct, (ii) holding on for reproduction that 'now' which is no more (Behaltenheit), and (iii) holding forth for recognition that 'now' which is not yet (Vorhaltenheit). It is only in terms of this three-fold distinction of time, which constitutes present, past and future, respectively, that the three-fold synthesis in question is possible. Further, it should be clear that these three distinctions of one and the same synthesis, must themselves form a unity. We must also say that in this unity future plays the leading or predominant role, for it is that which accounts for the character of self-sameness by means of recognition of itself.

It is this notion of time as the 'self-forming-self-receiving' unity which Heidegger calls the notion of original time, and identifies with the notion of transcendental imagination.

How does Kant look in the light of Heidegger's interpretation which I have given above? That is, what follows from it with regard to Kant's attempt to found the possibility of synthetic *a priori* propositions? In the first instance, it is clear that we do not have now two different faculties of sensibility and understanding which would have to be conjoined by transcendental imagination, but only one faculty of transcendental imagination itself with the dual role of sensibility and understanding. Without for the present going into whether Heidegger was right in thus reducing the two faculties in question, especially the latter, into one, it can at least be said, as I have pointed out before also, that such a reduction was necessary if they had to be essentially related to each other for the possibility of synthetic *a priori* propositions. In the second instance, insofar as Heidegger contends that the transcendental imagination is identical with what he calls original time, time must be said to be the ultimate basis of knowledge that we are seeking: that is, must constitute the definition of that self in respect of which we are essentially related to an object, i.e. of transcendence. Those who are familiar with Heidegger's main work, *Sein und Zeit,* as well as his other works, would not find it difficult to see that with his interpretation of transcendence as original time, Heidegger has brought Kant to a point where his own philosophy dwells. Substitute the word 'Dasein' for the word 'transcendence', and one already sees how much of it is Heidegger. As a matter of fact, the last part of his Kant book is solely devoted to the elaboration of his own philosophy as starting from this point. But it may be asked: is such an interpretation justified? That is, how far is Heidegger justified in reducing both sensibility and understanding, especially the latter, to transcendental imagination? How far is he justified in identifying transcendental imagination with time or original time? Moreover, how far is he justified in claiming, as he does in his above-mentioned book, that *all* synthetic *a priori* propositions are possible in terms of transcendental imagination?

In the following part of the paper I will be concerned with (i) showing that not all synthetic *a priori* propositions can be possible in terms of transcendental imagination as identified with Heidegger's notion of original time. That is, I would like to show that this notion can at best explain the possibility of synthetic *a priori* propositions of only what we may here loosely call metaphysics but not of ethics as Heidegger claims. For it seems to me that the nature of the ethical problem is such that it cannot have anything to do with this notion of time;

(ii) showing that it is doubtful whether it is in accordance with Kant's intention to reduce at least understanding to transcendental imagination. And there is reason to say, as I have shown above also, that understanding can have an independent existence apart from sensibility. Whatever the consequences of its irreducibility, its reducibility in the Heideggerian sense does not seem to be warranted from Kant himself; and finally,

(iii) stating at a greater length, without examining whether it can be identified with transcendental imagination, Heidegger's notion of original time.

(a) Heidegger's notion of original time and the question of the possibility of ethical knowledge

In his *Critique of Pure Reason*, the work with which we have been mainly concerned in this paper, Kant aims at the critique or what we might call explication of pure theoretical reason with a view to provide us with the foundation of metaphysics, i.e. the synthetic *a priori* propositions involved in it. He uses the term metaphysics in two different senses: to mean, firstly, that science which deals with the three notions of God, Freedom and Immortality. According to him, these notions are transcendent or super-empirical, and may therefore be said to form the subject-matter of that part of human reason which is transcendent or dialectical or (from the empirical point of view) illusory. Heidegger uses the term *metaphysics specialis* for this sense of metaphysics. Secondly, he uses the term metaphysics for that science which deals with the whole of pure theoretical reason. He uses the term *metaphysics generalis* for this other sense of metaphysics.

As distinguished from pure theoretical reason in the above-mentioned *Critique*, Kant uses the term pure practical reason in his *Critique of Practical Reason* and other of his ethical notes and writings to indicate that part of human reason which provides us with the foundation of ethics, i.e., the synthetic *a priori* propositions involved in it. If this is so, it may easily be opined that so far in our paper, as confining ourselves to a certain part of the former *Critique* and Heidegger's interpretation of it, we have been able to show at best only the possibility of synthetic *a priori* propositions of metaphysics but not at any rate of ethics: for these we have not even once touched. However, before Heidegger came to identify transcendental imagination with his notion of original time in his book in question, he sought to show the essential dependence of pure practical reason, like that of sensibility and understanding before this, upon the former. It is immaterial for my purpose here to explain how he does it.[32] It is enough to say that in doing so, he may undoubtedly be interpreted as believing that his notion of original time is the foundation of *all* synthetic *a priori* propositions, i.e. not merely those of metaphysics, but also those of ethics. I would like to show in this section that transcendental imagination, as identical with this notion of time, can make possible at best only the synthetic *a priori* propositions of metaphysics but not at any rate those of ethics.[33]

We have seen that Heidegger's notion of transcendental imagination as original time signifies that we have a capacity in ourselves to relate ourselves essentially (universally and necessarily) to an object, in such a manner that we receive and in the same process form it in three different ways. These ways, which obviously are merely three different aspects of one and the same activity, are synthesis in terms of (i) 'now which is there', (ii) 'now which is no more' and (iii) 'now which is not yet', that is, in terms of the three modes of time, namely present, past and future, with the final mode as playing the leading role.

The question which arises here is: what does this notion of time have to do with pure practical reason? It must be confessed that there is very little in Heidegger's works generally where one would discover a sufficient or satisfactory account of the ethical problem, which, as we have seen, is the same as that of practical reason. There are only a few stray notes about it here and there.[34] And from these it is difficult to gather or make out how he proposes to relate it with his notion of time, which, as I have said before, forms the crux of not merely his interpretation of Kant but also his own entire philosophical position. Even granting that pure practical reason, as accounting for that which we ought to do, has essentially to do with his notion of Being (Sein) in the sense of Dasein or transcendence[35] as essentially relating man to his objects in a certain way, it is difficult to see how this Being, interpreted as original time, could have anything to do with pure practical reason. In this respect Kant's attempt to explain man, i.e. man's transcendence (or Being), in terms of both his pure theoretical reason and pure practical reason, as accounting for metaphysics and ethics, respectively, certainly seems to be more plausible.

The objection that I have in mind is this. Time, as consisting of the three above-mentioned modes of present, past and future, can account only for those objects which have the time-character, that is to say, which in some sense *are*. This means that it can account only for the objects of metaphysics in either of its two senses. It cannot account for anything which does not have this character, and which in that sense, as we may say, *is not,* but which has the character of ought. This means to say that it cannot account for ethics. It is needless to point out here that there is a fundamental difference between the two cases, and that it was certainly due to this that Kant was led to distinguish between pure theoretical reason, on the one hand, and pure practical reason on the other, as two different modes of knowledge.[36] In more recent times Moore has affirmed this difference in his *Principia Ethica,* by contending that if we identify the two cases or try to show a relation of inference between them, then we commit what he calls the naturalistic fallacy, namely the fallacy of confusing what is ethical with something which is not so, i.e. which is factual or natural or even metaphysical (transcendent in Kant's sense).

It follows, therefore, that even if Heidegger's notion of original time succeeds in founding the synthetic *a priori* propositions of metaphysics in any of its two senses, it cannot succeed in doing so with regard to those of ethics.

(b) Transcendental imagination and understanding

In the first part of this paper I have shown that, according to Kant, understanding is an independent faculty, which has nothing essentially to do with sensibility. I pointed out that it was due to this reason that the problem of the relationship between the two faculties arose, and that one had to look for a competent mediator in transcendental imagination or original time as the case might be. It is obvious that if this were not so, the plan of the *Critique of Pure Reason* would be considerably altered, e.g. the chapter on Transcendental Deduction would become unnecessary, and large parts of the two books of Transcendental Analytic, namely Analytic of Concepts and Analytic of Principles, could not stand in their present form.[37] If Heidegger's contention with regard to the identification of understanding and transcendental imagination were true, then, these two would certainly have to be rewritten in the form of one book only with an identical subject-matter.

In the light of this thesis of the independence of understanding in Kant, Heidegger's attempt to identify it with transcendental imagination certainly looks like begging the question of Transcendental Deduction, namely the question about its relationship with sensibility.[38] What is it that leads Heidegger to do so? What evidence for it does he find in the *Critique of Pure Reason*? I have said that Kant undoubtedly meant to take understanding as an independent faculty, and that it is on this basis that his main critical work is planned as it is. We may say that it is only with regard to its relationship with sensibility that it can be considered as identical with transcendental imagination, but that is not the only function which it has. Besides its application to the latter it can exist as an empty form, that is to say, as form which, in Kant's words, can be thought though not known. Therefore, it seems clear that, in identifying understanding with transcendental imagination, Heidegger was unwarrantedly eliminating its function which it has over and above the latter and thus almost denying that there was any question to discuss in Transcendental Deduction.

I do not mean to say here that Kant was justified in considering understanding to be an independent faculty. And I am still undecided whether it could be completely identified with transcendental imagination. But it does seem clear to me that if it were considered independent, as Kant does so, then it would be impossible to think of it and sensibility as forming a transcendental unity, which, as we have seen, alone can give us synthetic *a priori* propositions. I have contended above that if they, and whatever else, have to form a unity, then they must be considered as one and the same faculty each with a dual role. In this respect, it must be confessed that, in reducing understanding to transcendental imagination, Heidegger was doing just that which alone could ensure us the required unity. Only it was not warranted by anything in Kant, and thus it meant skipping the problem in view.

Here it may be asked; is then there no solution to Kant's problem in the Transcendental Deduction? That is, must sensibility and understanding always stand separated from each other, and thus make the foundation of synthetic *a priori* propositions (of metaphysics in any of its two senses) always impossible for Kant? As it is it seems to be so.

(c) Heidegger's notion of original time

I have said before that I do not understand clearly Kant's notion of transcendental imagination. But from what we have seen above with regard to Heidegger's interpretation of it, it at least becomes clear that, in being identical with sensibility, it must be identical with the universal form of time. The question which might arise here is whether time, i.e. the universal form of time itself, in being identical with it, can take over the job of understanding as well. Besides the fact that it, i.e. time, in being a moment of one and the same unity, must do so, in interpreting the synthesis of recognition in terms of futurity (Vorhaltenheit), Heidegger tries to show that it does and can do it.

Now, I do not find myself in a position to examine whether time can play this dual role of both sensibility and understanding, As I have pointed out above, this conception of the nature of time plays a dominant role in the whole of Heidegger's philosophy. In what follows I shall use this opportunity to state at a greater length his notion of original time as distinguished from what he considers to be derivative time as understood in physics or mathematics. In doing so I shall draw from his works generally.

As I have pointed out just now and also explained to some extent before, Heidegger does not understand by his notion of original time that time which we use in physics or mathematics, namely a series of moments or 'nows' stretched continuously to infinity. According to him, this latter time is derivative. At present I will not try to show how he considers it to be so. I will simply be concerned with showing what his notion of the former is.

According to Heidegger, time, or what he calls original time is purely subjective; in Kantian phraseology we may say that it is the universal form of human subjectivity. However, the term subjectivity here does not mean as pertaining to an isolated subject, i.e. subject as isolated from an object to which it might or might not relate itself, i.e. a monad. For Heidegger there is nothing like that: such a notion for him is an abstraction. On the contrary, for him, a subject is essentially, i.e. universally and necessarily, related to its object, not this or that object but the Kantian object in general = x or what he also paradoxically calls Nothing. In other words, time is always naturally transcending itself to its object. Thus we may say that subjectivity is of the nature of transcendence. It follows from this that time, as the universal form of human subjectivity, is the universal form of transcendence. It is transcendence.

What does the notion of time as transcendence do? That is, what does it mean to say that transcendental subjectivity (if I may use that expression) is of the nature of time, or has it as its universal form? Again we must get our clue from Kant. To say that time is transcendence or that transcendental subjectivity is of the nature of time means that whenever we relate ourselves to our object (object in general = x or Nothing) we do so in the form of time. We may also express ourselves differently by saying that, as transcendence, time produces its own horizon for its object (and when we use the word 'produce' how near we are to understanding Heidegger's identification of time with transcendental imagination). In this sense we may say that it is self-transcendence. Or it is that which produces itself. Time produces itself (Zeit zeitigt sich). That undoubtedly is the meaning of time as transcendence for Heidegger.

Now, as transcendence, time produces or externalizes itself into its three different modes which form a unity. This means to say that the unity of time or transcendence—and unity it is no doubt—manifests itself, functions, so to say, in three different manners, which Heidegger very strikingly and also perhaps appropriately calls its ecstasies. These are present, past and future. I have already explained in short how these come into being, and how the last of them plays the leading role in their unification, i.e., in the unification of time. I have also pointed out before that it is this unity of the three modes of time, with future as the leading mode, which Heidegger calls original time, and from which, according to him, the physical or mathematical notion of time is derived.

It is clear that if this notion of original time is what defines transcendence for Heidegger, it is sure to be considered the sole foundation of *all* synthetic *a prori* propositions. I think we can leave our present discussion at that.

Notes

1. Translated by Norman Kernp Snith, *Macmillan,* London, 1953
2. *Vittorio Klostermann,* Frankfurt am Main, 1951
3. I shall, however, note here that if we deny the possibility of synthetic *a priori* propositions, then, as would be clear in the following, we would be denying the possibility of any knowledge whatsoever.
4. It should be noted that, merely for the reason that we search for these ways or manners in the nature of the subject itself, they are not mere psychological acts. In fact, nothing would be farther from the truth than to suppose that they are so. In my view such a supposition would betray complete lack of understanding of the whole problem of synthetic *a priori* propositions.

   Now, the ways or manners, which we are in search of and which we require to account for the possibility of synthetic *a priori* propositions, differ from any act of Psychology in two different ways. Firstly, they are not, like the acts of Psychology, a subject-matter of an empirical science. I have sufficiently emphasized above that synthetic *a priori* propositions, if they are at all possible, have nothing whatsoever to do with empirical or synthetic *a posteriori* propositions. Secondly—and this is the most important point for the understanding of the problem of synthetic *a priori* propositions—unlike the acts of Psychology, they tell us of a subject's own ways or manners of relating itself to an object without an object being there, i.e., they show how a subject is constituted with regard to any object whatsoever, or what Kant calls an object in general = x. To use an expression from Heidegger, they show how a subject is of the nature of transcendence (*KPM*, pp. 24–26), i.e. object-related.

5. It should be clear from what is said here that, for Kant, sensibility is not the same thing as senses. Senses give us empirical sensations or intuitions; sensibility does not. Sensibility is merely mind's capacity to receive an object without actually receiving it. Senses actually receive an object. One must even say that senses actually receive an object, because mind has the capacity of receiving any object whatsoever, i.e., because it has sensibility. It is not the other way round.
6. (a) Though, of course, existing in this manner an object would be without the advantage of the operation of understanding. This point would be clear as we proceed.
   (b) *CPR*, Transcendental Deduction (B).
7. *CPR*, p. 113.
8. By this is meant that for understanding, in order to be meaningful, there is only one sort of object to apply to, namely the object of sensibility. And this is so, because, firstly, mind has only one sort of object, namely the one which it receives through sensibility, and no other sort of object whatsoever; and secondly, understanding cannot create any object of its own. For this, i.e., for an object, it must depend upon sensibility, the only faculty of giving or receiving an object.
9. *CPR*, Transcendental Deduction (B).
10. Words in square brackets our own.
11. *CPR*, p. 182 (A), also p. 174 (A) and pp. 181–82 (A).
12. Words in square brackets our own.
13. *CPR*, p. 198.
14. Words in square brackets our own.
15. *CPR*, p. 200.
16. *CPR*, pp. 201–3.

17. Cf. Hermann Mörchen's 'Die Einbildungskraft bei Kant' in *Jahrbuch für Philosophie und phänomenologische Forschung*, volume XI, 1930, for the lack of any clear-cut conception of Einbildungskraft in Kant's *CPR*.
18. "In der Tat ist die Frage nach der Einbildungskraft bei Kant zunächst eine Verlgenheitsfrage." Mörchen's just-mentioned essay, p. 314.
19. As concerning the nature of man in essential relationship with an object, the problem of synthetic *a priori* propositions, according to Heidegger, is not, as has often been supposed, an epistemological, but an ontological, problem. (*KPM*, p. 25) He also calls it the problem of fundamental ontology. This expression is in consonance with his interpretation of the *Critique of Pure Reason* as providing the ground of metaphysics. (*KPM*, p. 13)

    According to Heidegger, the idea of the Copernican Revolution is the same as that of transcendence, namely that of man having to do with an object in an essential manner. (*KPM*, p. 26) Though he calls the problem of synthetic *a priori* propositions as that of fundamental ontology, he identifies fundamental ontology with what he calls ontological knowledge, as distinguished from the ontic one, meaning by the former that knowledge which is presupposed in all other knowledge.

    As such it seems to be only a matter of terminology whether we call the problem of synthetic *a priori* propositions an ontological or an epistemological one: what is meant in either case is the investigation of the nature or constitution of transcendence in the given sense.

    In this connection, cf. Ernst Cassirer's 'Kant und das Problem der Metaphysik – Bemerkungen zu Martin Heidegger's Kant-Interpretation, *Kant-Studien,* volume XXXVI. Cassirer contends that Kant's problem is epistemological.
20. *KPM*, p. 126.
21. *KPM*, p. 126.
22. *KPM*, p. 127.
23. *KPM*, p. 126.
24. *KPM*, pp. 163, 171, 172.
25. *KPM*, p. 131.
26. *KPM*, p. 138.
27. *KPM*, p. 130–3.
28. *KPM*, p. 162.
29. ". . . dass die Einbildungskraft nur ein Element unter anderen und keineswegs die Wurzel von Anschauung und Begriff ist. Das trifft zu."

30. "Dass die transcendentale Einbildungskraft die Wurzel von Sinnlichkeit und Verstand ist, hat freilich die ursprünglichere Auslegung dargetan. Von diesem Ergebnis soll hier kein Gebrauch gemacht werden. Vielmehr soll die Herausarbeitung des inneren Zeitcharakters der drei Modi der Synthesis den letzten entscheidenden Beweis dafür vorlegen, dass die Interpretation der transzendentalen Einbildungskraft als die Wurzel der beiden Stämme nicht nur möglich, sondern notwendig ist."
31. *CPR* p. 131, and *KPM*, p. 161.
32. *KPM*, pp. 143–6.
33. For a similar view, cf. Ernst Cassiers already mentioned essay, pp. 13, 17.
34. For example, *KPM*, pp. 143–46; and *Einführung in die Metaphysik*, pp. 149–52.
35. *Einführung in die Metaphysik*, p. 151
36. *CPR*, pp. 472–3: " 'Ought' expresses a kind of necessity and of connection with grounds which is found nowhere else in the whole of nature. The understanding can know in nature only what is, what has been, or what will be. We cannot say that anything in nature *ought to be* other than what in all these time relations it actually is. When we have the course of nature alone in view *'ought'* has no meaning whatsoever. It is just as absurd to ask what ought to happen in the natural world as to ask what properties a circle ought to have. All that we are justified in asking is: what happens in nature? What are the properties of the circle?"
37. And what will happen to Transcendental Dialectic? Cf, Ernst Cassirer's above-mentioned essay, p. 11, as well as R. Oderbrecht's 'Martin Heideggers Kant und das *Problem der Metaphysik*, *Blätter für deutsche Philosophy*, volume 5, p. 133. It is strange that Heidegger completely leaves out this section of *CPR* from his Kant-Interpretation.
38. Eberhard Griesbach, in his 'Interpretation oder Destruktion? Zum kritischen Verständnis von Martin Heideggers Kant und das Problem der Metaphysik', *Deutsche Vierteljahresschrift für Literaturwissenschaft und Geisteswissenschaft*, volume VIII, calls Heidegger's attempt "die Errichtung einer philosophischen Diktatur" oder eine "Vergewaltigung."

    A similar view has been taken by Heinrich Levy in his 'Heideggers Kantinterpretation. Zu Heideggers Buch Kant und das Problem der Metaphysik', *Logos*, volume XXI, p. 8.

    "Auch in dieser Kantinterpretation—und das muss in Hinblick auf die ausgedehnte Kritik, die sie unterworfen wird vorausgeschickt werden—zeigt sich die Kuhnheit und Durchdachtheit des Entwurfs, die gesammelte Energie des Systematikers, der sein Ziel nie aus den Augen verliert, der von seiner Idee durchdrungen, bei aller Aporetik allerdings dogmatische Philosoph, der durch die verwickeltesten Gedankengänge hindurch in Einbildungskraft—die Kraft, eine Konstruktion hineinzubilden—sich nicht an dem unmittelbaren (wenn auch nicht unvermittelten) Stoff aller Philosophic, sondern an dem Werk, das einer der grössten Denker aus ihm geformt hat, an einer bereits vollzogenen ausgeprägten begrifflichen Sinndeutung die sich nicht durch Interpretation in eine ihr wesentlich heterogene verwandeln lässt."

2

Wittgenstein's Theory of 'Family Resemblances' in his *Philosophical Investigations* (Secs. 65–80)

1. In the first 64 sections of his *Philosophical Investigations,* Wittgenstein is chiefly concerned with showing the inadequacy of what may be called the Reference Theory of Meaning and with replacing it with his own Use Theory of Meaning.

(1) He reads off the first kind of theory from the quotation from Augustine's *Confessions,* 1.8, which he mentions in section 1, and which he states as maintaining that (i) every word in language names or means a specific object, and (ii) a sentence is a combination of such words. (Sec. 1) He takes his own theory of meaning in his *Tractatus Logico-Philosophicus* as illustrative of this kind of theory. (Sec. 23) One of his main objections against this theory is that it is restricted, not complete; it describes just one meaning of language, not its other meanings.

> "Augustine, we might say, does describe a system of communication; only not everything that we call language is this system. And one has to say this in many cases where the question arises "Is this an appropriate description or not?" The answer is: "Yes, it is appropriate, but only for this narrowly circumscribed region, not for the whole of what you were claiming to describe."

It is as if someone were to say: "A game consists in moving objects about on a surface according to certain rules. . . ." — and we replied: You seem to be thinking of board games, but there are others. You can make your definition correct by expressly restricting it to those games." (Sec. 3)

(2) According to Wittgenstein's own Use Theory of Meaning, a large class of words and sentences have a multiplicity of meanings, depending upon their different uses or functions in different given contexts, in different given language-games. Thus, for example, in section 33, he indicates a few of the various uses, and consequently meanings, of the word 'blue' in different language-games:

> "Is this blue the same as the blue over there? Do you see any difference?"
> You are mixing and you say "It is hard to get the blue of this sky".
> "It is turning fine, you can already see blue sky again".
> "Look what different effects these two blues have".
> "Do you see the blue over there? Bring it here."
> "This blue signal-light means. . . ."
> "What's blue called? — Is it 'indigo'?"

In sections 11–12, Wittgenstein compares words and sentences with tools:

> "Think of the tools in a tool-box: there is a hammer, pliers, a saw, a screw-driver, a rule, a glue-pot, glue, nails and screws. — The functions of words are as diverse as the functions of these objects. (And in both cases there are similarities).
> Of course, what confuses us is the uniform appearance of words when we hear them spoken or meet them in script and print. For their *application* is not presented to us so clearly. Especially not, when we are doing philosophy !" (Sec. 11)
> "It is like looking into the cabin of a locomotive. We see handles all looking more or less alike. (Naturally, since they

> are all supposed to be handled.) But one is the handle of a crank which can be moved continuously (it regulates the opening of a valve); another is the handle of a switch, which has only two effective positions, it is either off or on; a third is the handle of a brake-lever, the harder one pulls on it, the harder it brakes; a fourth the handle of a pump: it has an effect only so long as it is moved to and fro." (Sec. 12)

2. In sections 65–80, with which alone I am concerned here and which contain his theory of 'family resemblances', Wittgenstein is no more concerned with a *semantic* problem as of the earlier sections, the semantic problem of the meaning of a word or a sentence in a given language, or of what unites the different paradigms of the uses of a word or a sentence, or with some other similar problem. On the contrary, his problem now is primarily a *metaphysical* problem, the metaphysical problem of the subsumption of several objects under one and the same head or under one and the same word in *one* of its many possible uses, the metaphysical problem of the nature (as distinguished from the status) of a concept or universal.

> "Here we come up against the great question that lies behind all these considerations. — For someone might object against me: "You take the easy way out! You talk about all sorts of language-games, but have nowhere said, what the essence of a language-game, and hence of language, is: what is common to all these activities, and what makes them into language or parts of language. So you let yourself off the very part of the investigation that once gave you yourself most headache, the part about the *general form of propositions* and of language." (Sec. 65)

Wittgenstein's theory of 'family resemblances' is his theory of the nature of a concept. Briefly speaking, according to this theory, a concept, like the concept of language or the concept of game, is not to be defined, as has traditionally been done, with reference to a class, i.e., with reference to a characteristic or characteristics said to belong in *common* to *all* the members of a given set of objects. On the other hand, a concept is to be defined with reference to a family/'family resemblances', i.e., with reference to characteristics some of which may belong in *common* to *some* members of a given set of objects and some others to *some* other members of that set of objects, in some such way as follows:— Given a set of objects 'ABCDEF', c_1 may belong to 'ABCD', c_2 may belong to 'BCDE', and c_3 may belong to 'CDEF'. According to Wittgenstein, all of the objects 'ABCDEF' are subsumed under one and the same head by virtue of such resemblances amongst them, which he calls 'family resemblances', and not by virtue of something allegedly belonging in common to all these objects.

> ". . . Instead of producing something common to all that we call language, I am saying that these phenomena have no one thing in common which makes us use the same word for all, — but that they are related to one another in many different ways. And it is because of this relationship, or these relationships, that we call them all "language". I will try to explain this (Sec. 65).
>
> "Consider for example the proceedings that we call "games". I mean board-games, card-games, ball-games, Olympic games, and so on. What is common to them all? — Don't say: "There *must* be something common, or they would not be called 'games'" — but look and see whether there is anything common to all. — For if you look at them you will not see something that is common to *all*, but similarities, relationships, and a whole series of them at that. To repeat: don't think, but look! — Look for example at board-games, with their multifarious relationships. Now pass to card-games: here you find many correspondences with the first group, but many common features drop out, and others appear. When we pass next to ball-games, much that is common is retained, but much is lost, — Are they all 'amusing'? Compare chess with noughts and crosses. Or is there always winning and losing, or competition between

> players? Think of patience. In ball-games there is winning and losing, but when a child throws his ball at the wall and catches it again, this feature has disappeared. Look at the parts played by skill and luck; and at the difference between skill in chess and skill in tennis. Think now of games like ring-a-ring-a-roses, here is the element of amusement, but how many other characteristic features have disappeared! And we can go through the many, many other groups of games in the same way; can see how similarities crop up and disappear.
>
> "And the result of this examination is: we see a complicated network of similarities overlapping and criss-crossing: sometimes overall similarities, sometimes similarities of detail." (Sec. 66)
>
> "I can think of no better expression to characterize these similarities than 'family resemblances', for the various resemblances between members of a family, build, features, colour of eyes, gait, temperament, etc. etc. overlap and criss-cross in the same way. — And I shall say: 'games' form a family," (Secs. 67)

Wittgenstein concedes that his view of the nature of a concept will give us a blurred concept. But he maintains that a blurred concept is quite usable (Secs, 69–71 and 75).

3. Now, in examining Wittgenstein's just mentioned 'family resemblances' view of the nature of a concept, I would like to begin with taking some samples of concepts, so current in Wittgenstein himself, and mentioning respectively characteristic or characteristics which I believe to be not only *common* but also *peculiar* to *all* the objects subsumed under those concepts. Since I believe these characteristics to be both common and peculiar to all the objects respectively subsumed under the given concepts, I may formulate about them the following questions, as criteria: (1) Would one include under a given concept an object which possessed these characteristics? (2) Would one exclude

from that concept an object which did not possess these characteristics? If the answers to both these questions are in the affirmative, then, one may naturally be quite sure that the characteristics in question are both common and peculiar to all the objects respectively subsumed under the given concepts.

Consider the following:

Family = A unit of social organization consisting of a husband/husbands and their wife/wives, or these and their children.

Concept = Comprehension of a set of objects under one and the same head by virtue of some resemblance or resemblances found amongst them.

Language (in the widest sense) = A natural or an artificial means of communication, i.e. a sign or a symbol.

Game = "An occupation which is pleasant for its own sake" (Spiel ist eine "Beschäftigung, die für sich angenehm ist".

"Bei der Arbeit ist die Beschäftigung nicht an selbst angenehm, sondern man unternimmt sie einer anderen Absicht wegen. Die Beschäftigung bei dem Spiele dagegen ist an sich angenehm, ohne weiter irgendeinen Zweck zu beabsichtigen" Kant),

On the whole, although without being exhaustive and more as mentioning some wide-ranging illustrations, one may say that there are in the world:

(1) Objects which we take or produce as means to an end, like, to take some of Wittgenstein's own examples, games, artificial languages, handles. The concept of any of these different sets of objects, as has just been seen in the case of games and artificial languages, is the comprehension of their specific utility. These objects may be said to constitute *artificial* classes.

(2) There are objects, which we do not take or produce as means to an end, but which we encounter, like human

beings, horses, mountains. It is indeed possible to mention respectively characteristics which are both common and peculiar to these different sets of objects. Take, for example, Aristotle's highly plausible definition of man, constructed *per genus et differentiam,* as a rational animal; or the existentialistic no less plausible definition of man, constructed in the same Aristotelian manner, as a being in whom existence precedes essence. These objects may be said to constitute *real* classes.

(3) There are objects, which we do not take or produce as a means to an end, nor which do we encounter, but which we imagine, like mermaids, fairies, unicorns. It is undeniably easily possible to mention respectively characteristics both common and peculiar to these different sets of objects. These objects may be said to constitute *imaginary* classes.

4. I have just contended against Wittgenstein's 'family resemblances' view of the nature of a concept that a concept can be defined with reference to a class. I have done this through actually defining some specific concepts in that manner, and through throwing light on some classes of concepts which can also be defined in that manner. My second objection against Wittgenstein's view is: Can we at all define a concept with reference to a family/'family resemblances', without confusing it in each single case with some other concept or concepts? For given two sets of objects, 'ABCDEF and 'UVWXYZ', a characteristic (or characteristics) which is said to belong to 'ABCD of the first set, may well and does indeed also belong to 'UVWX' of the second set. Thus, for example, take games. According to Wittgenstein, 'winning and losing', 'skill', 'luck' are characteristics of some of the games, not of others, but then, are they not also the characteristics of fights and battles and so many of other of life's activities? Similarly he believes 'amusement' to be a characteristic of some games, not of all, but again, is it not

also a characteristic of sadistic and masochistic activities and of so much else? The same would be the case with other concepts.

As a result, we would not only have no blurred concept, we would have no concept whatsoever which we could even more or less safely use.

5. The third and the last point which I wish to make is that, although Wittgenstein maintains that a concept is to be defined with reference to a family/'family resemblances', he does not, so far as one can see, actually define *any* concept in that manner. That is, he does not mention any set of 'family resemblances' which would define a given concept. Even his account of games in section 66 which I have deliberately reproduced above inspite of its general familiarity, and which is the most elaborate account of the nature of a concept that he mentions, is more illustrative than definitive.

It may be said, in defence of Wittgenstein, that we know a concept in *use,* that is, we know *practically* what for example games are. But the fact that we know this, if it always be a fact, does not so much depend upon our knowing it with reference to a family or to a class, whatever else it might depend upon. And were the choice to fall between the two disputed alternatives, then, it would more likely fall on the latter alternative than on the former: that is, for example, on being asked why in cases 'ABCDEF' he thought that the people were playing games, the person concerned would more likely say something like: 'The fellows were enjoying themselves, weren't they!' than mention any criss-cross resemblances, "twist fibre on fibre".

6. I may sum up my conclusions as follows: In respect of Wittgenstein's *metaphysical* 'family resemblances' thesis of the nature of a concept in sections 65–80, as distinguished from his *semantic* use thesis of the nature of meaning of words and sentences in a given language in the earlier sections, I have argued: (1) that a concept can be defined with reference to a class, (2) that a concept cannot be defined with reference to a family/

'family resemblances', without confusing it with some other concept or concepts, and (3) that Wittgenstein himself, so far as one can see, does not actually define *any* concept in that manner, including the concept of games which he elaborates at length.

3

Kant's Definition of an Analytic Proposition

IN THE IV portion of the Introduction of his *Critique of Pure Reason*, the portion entitled 'The Distinction between Analytic and Synthetic Judgements', Kant defines, as I understand it, an analytic judgement or proposition in four interchangeable ways[1]. I may state these four ways as follows: (1) An analytic proposition is one in which the predicate is already contained in the subject. (2) An analytic proposition is one in which the predicate is related to the subject through identity (undoubtedly in the sense of being partially or wholly identical with the subject). (3) An analytic proposition is one in which the predicate does not add anything to the subject but simply breaks it up or analyses it into its component parts. It is for this reason that Kant also calls an analytic proposition explicative. (4) An analytic proposition is one in which one extracts the predicate from the subject "in accordance with the principle of contradiction".[2] This point is made more explicitly when in Book II, Chapter II, Section I entitled, 'The Highest Principle of all Analytic Judgements', of his *Critique of Pure Reason*, Kant says "... if the *judgement* is *analytic* ... its truth can always be adequately known in accordance with the principle of contradiction. The reverse of that which as concept is contained and is thought in the knowledge of the object, is always rightly denied. But since the opposite of the concept would contradict the object, the concept itself must necessarily be affirmed of it", and, in continuation, "*The Principle* of *contradiction* must therefore be recognized as being the universal and completely sufficient principle of all analytic knowledge . . .".[3] I may express all this briefly by saying that an analytic proposition is one the denial of which would be self-contradictory. In opposition to these four ways in which Kant defines an analytic proposition, he may be said to define a synthetic proposition as one in which the predicate lies outside the subject, in which the predicate is related to the subject without identity, in which the predicate does not simply explicate the subject but adds something to it or which is ampliative, and the denial of which would not be self-contradictory. Kant mentions 'All bodies are extended' as an example of an analytic proposition, and 'All bodies are heavy' as an example of a synthetic proposition.

It is not at all difficult to see how the four ways in which Kant defines an analytic proposition are interchangeable. Let us explain this, even perhaps at the expense of a certain amount of redundancy, by means of an entirely simple and straightforward example. Take the proposition 'A brother is a male' (we could just as well take the proposition 'A brother is a male sibling'). Now, quite evidently, we could express this proposition in any of the four following ways with absolutely no change in meaning. We could say that, in this proposition, the predicate concept of 'being a male' is already contained or included in, or is a part and parcel of the subject concept of 'being a brother', the former is already an element in the constitution of the latter. Or, we could say that in this proposition, 'being a male' is partially identical with 'being a brother', is identical with a part of the latter complex. Or, we could say that, in this proposition, 'being a male' does not add anything to 'being a brother', does not provide any new information about it, any information which is not already embodied in it, but simply makes explicit one of its (covert) constituents. Or, we could say that the denial of the predicate concept of 'being a male' to the subject concept of 'being a brother' would be self-contradictory, i.e. the proposition

'A brother is not a male' would be self-contradictory. In short, we could express the proposition 'A brother is a male', with absolutely no alteration in meaning, through the concept of Containment, or Identity, or Reiteration or Explication, or Non-Contradiction.

Now, all this (namely Kant's definition of an analytic proposition in any of the four forms which I have mentioned and which I have found to be interchangeable) seems to be clear and, in respect of propositions of at least one particular kind, convincing enough. There are innumerable propositions, like the one which I have mentioned in the preceding paragraph and all of which may be symbolized as '(a + b) is (a + b)'or '(a + b) is (a/b)', to which Kant's definition of an analytic proposition in any of its various forms is entirely applicable. However that may be, in his 'Two Dogmas of Empiricism', Quine considers Kant's definition of an analytic proposition only in terms of Containment and criticizes it on two grounds: that it limits itself to propositions of the subject -predicate form, and that it makes use of a notion of containment which is left at a metaphorical level. Similarly, in his book *Kant,* Körner also takes up Kant's definition only in terms of Containment and criticizes it for the same two reasons as Quine, adding only that as being metaphorical Kant's definition is too vague.[5] But he goes on to say, "Although both objections are justified, I do not believe either is so serious as may seem at first sight. It is perfectly true that the subject of a judgement cannot contain its predicate in the same sense in which one box can contain another. But Kant's meaning is clear: the subject of a judgement *contains* its predicate, if, and only if, the negation of the judgement is a contradiction in terms. To say metaphorically that in the judgment 'Green is a colour', 'colour' is contained in 'green' is merely to say that by denying of green that it is a colour we are contradicting ourselves".[6] And as to the charge of Kant's defintion limiting itself to the subject-predicate form of proposition Körner maintains that this definition can be extended to cover other forms of proposition as well ". . . the denial of a proposition may be a contradiction in terms even if the proposition is not of subject-predicate form. For example, the denial of 'if *a* is greater than *b* then *b* is smaller than *a*' is certainly a contradiction in terms. The proposition on the other hand does not tell us anything that is not 'contained' in its terms".[7] Körner adds that this definition of an analytic proposition, whether in the subject-predicate form or any other form as one, non-metaphorically speaking, the denial of which would be a contradiction in terms 'or, what amounts to the same, which is *logically* necessary or, again in other words, the negation of which is *logically* impossible', as distinguished from a synthetic proposition which is any proposition which is not analytic, is accepted by contemporary logicians almost generally, although, he concedes, this distinction "is not wholly unproblematic or as unproblematic as I shall assume it to be"[8].

My purpose at present is not to consider the charge of Kant's limitation of his definition of an analytic proposition to the subject-predicate form of proposition nor Körner's suggestion that this definition may be extended to cover other forms of proposition as well. Dogmatically speaking, both the criticism and Körner's suggestion would seem to be justified. Attempts have been made to explain Kant's limitation of his definition to the subject-predicate form of proposition by means of his acceptance or alleged acceptance of traditional logic which dealt mainly with such propositions. In any case, what I wish to do here is to consider the charge of Kant's definition of an analytic proposition being metaphorical and, as Körner maintains, "therefore too vague". I will ignore the fact of Quine's confining himself to Kant's definition in terms of Containment and his overlooking his definition in other terms. I will also ignore the fact of Körner again confining himself to the same form of definition, his translation of this form of definition which he calls metaphorical and "therefore too vague" into the form of definition in terms of non-contradiction which he calls non-metaphorical and which he, surprisingly, shows no sign of recognizing in Kant himself, and his once again overlooking not only this latter form of definition but also the other two remaining forms of Kant's definition. I will discuss here the criticism of Kant's definition of an analytic proposition in terms of Containment which I wish to deal with at present through a treatment of the following two questions: (1) Is Kant's definition metaphorical? and (2) Granting that it is metaphorical, what exactly is wrong with its being so? Is it, just by virtue of its being metaphorical, 'too vague', as Körner contends?

It would seem that, according to Körner, the notion of conceptual containment (containment, say, of the predicate-concept in the subject-concept in an analytic proposition) is conceived on the analogy of the notion of physical containment (containment, say, of one box in another box), and is therefore metaphorical.[9] He, however, gives no reason for the thesis that the notion of physical containment is primary and that of conceptual containment patterned after it. Quine does not at all say why he considers Kant's definition metaphorical, but one suspects that his reasoning in this connection would not be any different from that of Körner, and would therefore be open to the same difficulty. The question which I would like to ask here is this: How to find out or determine that Kant's definition of an analytic proposition as one in which the predicate is *contained* in the subject is metaphorical? How to find out or determine that the concept of containment as used in this definition has been used metaphorically? It is possible to put this question more generally. It is already clear that the term 'contain' can be used in a physical context, as when one says that one box contains another box. It is also already clear that the term can be used in a conceptual context, as when Kant talks of the subject-concept containing the predicate-concept in an analytic proposition. In his article 'Kant's Analytic/Synthetic Distinction', Lucey, among numerous other contexts in which the terms under consideration can occur, specifically mentions four more contexts: "(A) Temporal Context: e.g., the month of February usually *contains* twenty-eight days. (B) Mathematical context: e.g., the series of natural numbers *contains* an infinite number of odd numbers.

(C) Set-theoretic context: e.g., the set of all philosophers that ever lived *contains* Plato, Aristotle, Kant and numerous others. (D) Auditory context: e.g., the closing bars of this symphony *contain* a subtle variation on the work's overall theme."[10] Now, our question, put more generally, is: How to find out or determine that the term 'contains' as used in one or more of a large number of contexts in which it can be used is primary and that the term as used in the remainder of these contexts is metaphorical?

Two of the ways, it seems to me, which one may adopt in order to answer this question are: (1) by an appeal to the dictionary, by following the lexical approach, and (2) by an appeal to usage, by following the usage approach. Now, a lexical survey of the relevant meanings of the term 'contain' and the relevant meanings of the terms which constitute the relevant meanings of that term i.e. a lexical survey of the term 'contain' in the relevant sense and the terms which are related to that term in that relevant sense, terms like 'include', 'enclose', 'comprise', 'comprehend', 'to have as a part (or the whole)', 'to have within', does not on the whole indicate anything to the effect that these terms as used in one or more of the various contexts in which they can be used are primary and as used in the remainder of those contexts are metaphorical. What this survey unmistakably points to is that all these related terms embody the idea of 'being or having within certain fixed limits', the idea of 'x having y as existing within its limits' or the idea of 'y existing within x' s limits', without any suggestion on the whole as to the nature of the objects x and y. Similarly a study of the usage of the term 'contain' has no different story to tell from what the foregoing lexical survey of that term has to say. (1) It shows that this term is used in a large variety of contexts. I have already mentioned some of these contexts, and many more can be added. (2) It does not show that the term as used in one or more of these contexts is primary and as used in the other of these contexts is metaphorical. (3) It shows that the term as used in all the various contexts in which it is used expresses the same common idea of 'being or having within certain fixed limits'. We have already seen that, according to Lucey, the term 'contain' can be used in very many contexts. He shows his agreement with my two latter propositions concerning the usage of that term as well, when he says that the term has pretty much the same meaning in all these contexts, namely 'to exist as fixed limits for': what merely varies from context to context is the kind of limit being referred to (one could have said, the kind of objects being referred to)[11]. It will follow from the preceding deliberations that as far as one can see, there is no case for saying that the term 'contain' as used in one or more of the contexts in which it can be used is primary and as used in the other of these contexts is metaphorical, and consequently no case for Quine's and Körner's contention that Kant's definition of an analytic proposition in terms of Containment is metaphorical. One wonders here whether, in considering the notion of physical containment as primary and that of conceptual containment as metaphorical, as it seems, Quine and Körner have not been misled by the picture which language may unwittingly arouse in us, whether there has not taken place a sort of Wittgensteinian bewitchment of language.

But suppose that Kant's definition of an analytic proposition as one in which the predicate term is contained in the subject term is metaphorical, that, say, the notion of conceptual containment involved in this definition is constructed on the analogy of the notion of physical containment. The question is: What exactly is wrong with its being so? Is it, simply by virtue of its being metaphorical, 'too vague', as Körner maintains? Let us take the proposition, symbolically expressed, "The term '(a + b)' *contains* the term '(a + b)'" or "The term '(a + b)' *contains* the term '(a/b),'" which for Kant would be an analytic propositon. Or let us take the more concrete proposition "The term 'brother' *contains* the term 'male sibling'" or "The term 'brother' *contains* the term 'male/sibling'", which again for Kant would be an analytic proposition. I for one, I am afraid, utterly fail to see any difficulty, anything vague, in these propositions. One could express these propositions differently as I have already partly done, and, I believe, non-metaphorically, if that would help in their further clarification, by saying that in them the predicate term forms, or constitutes a part or the whole of the subject term, i.e. in other words, that in them the predicate forms or constitutes a part or the whole of the meaning of the subject. It is unnecessary to add that one could also represent these propositions diagrammatically, should that again throw more light on them, as follows: by taking two circles to stand for the subject term (S) and the predicate term (P), one could schematize them (the propositions) by putting the smaller circle P inside the larger circle S or by having the circle P as coincident with the circle S. A corollary follows here: If the given propositions, assuming them to be metaphorical, are not confronted with any difficulty, are not vague, as I have just tried to show, then one could not object to any expression (including a defining expression) simply on the ground that it was metaphorical, one could not call it vague just because it happened to be metaphorical. One should no doubt expect the conceptual content of a metaphorical expression to be clearly and distinctly translatable into non-metaphorical terms. But that is an entirely different matter.

Notes

1. Kant's *Critique of Pure Reason,* translated by Norman Kemp Smith, *Macmillan,* 1953 reprint, pp. A6, A7, B10–B12.
2. *CPR,* A7, B12.
3. *CPR,* A151, B190–191.
4. *Clarity is not Enough,* edited by H. D. Lewis, *Allen and Unwin,* 1963, pp. 110–11.
5. S. Körner's *Kant,* Penguin, 1955, p. 22.
6. *Ibid.*
7. *Kant,* p. 23.
8. *Ibid.*
9. *Kant,* p. 23.
10. K.G. Lucey's 'Kant's Analytic/Synthetic Distinction', *Akten des 4. Internationalen Kant-Kongresses,* Teil III, *Walter de Gruyter,* Berlin 1974, p. 118.
11. Lucey's 'Kant's Analytic Synthetic Distinction', p. 119.

4

What is a Criterion? – Some Reflections

1. What exactly is this question about the nature of a criterion? What exactly are we looking for when we are looking for a criterion? Suppose, for example, the person A says that the person B is in pain, and the person C asks for A's criterion for saying what he says, then what exactly is C wishing to know? But is a criterion not simply that by which to judge that x, that something is such and such, that, for instance, A is in pain? Is it not simply a ground for, evidence in favour of identifying x? But then, is the meaning or definition of an object not also that by which to identify that object? Further, can one not identify an object by means of something which is more or less conjoined or correlated with it? And if so, how is a criterion distinguished from a definition, and from a correlate of an object functioning as a ground for identifying that object?

2. Now, suppose, to revert to our illustration, that A says that B is in pain, and we ask for A's criterion for saying what he says. The most likely answer, I imagine, would be, 'B's bodily behaviour'. But is it not possible for B to be in pain and yet not manifest that bodily behaviour which A takes as his criterion for judging B to be in pain, or for B to manifest that bodily behaviour and yet not to be in pain? And if so, would not A's criterion be a contingent criterion? But does the concept of a contingent criterion, a criterion which may not hold on occasions, make sense? Must a criterion not be a necessary criterion (does the concept

of a criterion not involve the requirement of being a necessary criterion)? That is, must it not be the case that whenever and wherever a criterion is there, the object for which it is a criterion must also be there, and whenever and wherever an object is there, whatever is its criterion must also be there? And in that case, would one not rather call A's 'criterion' by some other name, say, a sign or symptom?

3. If a criterion must be necessarily, not contingently, related to the object of which it is a criterion, what are the conditions under which alone it would be so related to that object (or, generally expressed, what are the conditions under which alone an object would be so related to another object)? Are there any more of these conditions except the following three: (1) that the criterion of an object constitutes the very meaning or definition of that object, that the criterion of an object and the meaning of that object are interchangeable terms or the proposition 'C—M' (where 'C' stands for a criterion of an object and 'M' for the meaning of that object) expresses an identical proposition; (2) that C logically follows from M, that C is related to M with analytic necessity or the proposition 'M—C' is an analytic *a priori* proposition; and (3) that C is related to the object of which it is a criterion with synthetic necessity or that the proposition 'O—C (where 'O' stands for the object of which 'C' is a criterion) is a synthetic *a priori* proposition?

Now, if a criterion must be necessarily related to the object of which it is a criterion, and if it can be necessarily related to that object only in the above-mentioned three ways, then, would it not follow that a criterion *could* only be one or more of these three things? It is obviously not said here which of these things *is* a criterion, whether it is definition or that which is deduced from definition or a necessary correlate of an object; what is said is only which of the things alone *could* be a criterion (namely one or more of the three things that I have mentioned).

4. But which of the three things *is* a criterion? However, could not an object be identified by any of these three things, by any of the things which are necessarily related to that object?

That is, is it not the case that, since all the three things under consideration are necessarily related to that object, whenever and wherever any of them is present the object must also be present, and *vice versa*, and therefore the presence of any of them could be taken as a ground for judging the presence of that object, as a criterion of that object?

One need not illustrate how the definition of an object could be a ground for identifying that object. The definition of an object embodies the essential nature of that object, so that an object could not be other than what its definition makes it out to be. I may, however, illustrate how that which logically follows from the definition of an object, or a necessary correlate of an object, could be grounds for identifying that object. Suppose, for example, that from the concept, or whatever comprehends the essential nature, of good in itself it logically follows, as it indeed does, that a thing which is good in itself would still be good even if it existed in complete isolation from everything else (that such a thing, even if it were left alone, 'would still shine like a jewel for its own sake as something which has its full value in itself).' Then, 'a thing's continuing to be good even if it found itself in a state of complete isolation' could be taken as a ground for identifying it as a thing good in itself

It would be dogmatic to simply mention an example of that which is connected with an object with synthetic necessity. For to do so would be already to commit ourselves to one particular approach in the controversy over the possibility of synthetic *a priori* propositions. But I may take here an example of the required kind tentatively. Suppose that the concept of duty is different from that of good but is so connected with it that whenever and wherever there is something which is good this thing is necessarily also one which it is one's duty to bring into existence, and *vice versa*. Then, 'a thing's being one's duty to realize' could be taken as a ground for identifying that thing as one which is good.

Would it not follow from these deliberations that definition is just one of the species of criterion, one of the grounds on which, or one form of evidence by which, to judge that x?

5. If an object were completely independent, quite unrelated to any other object, then we could not obviously take as its criterion anything other than its definition or some corollary of that definition. There are in that sense no independent criteria of any object. And I have earlier wondered whether an object which is not necessarily but only contingently related to a given object could be taken as a criterion of that object. Thus, on the whole, it seems, X would be a criterion of an object O if and only if, (1) X constitutes the definition of O, or (2) X logically follows from the definition of O, or (3) X is related to O necessarily but synthetically. I have said earlier that if X is contingently related to O, then X would be rather a sign or symptom of O. It follows from the above that if X is totally unrelated to O, is neither necessarily nor contingently related to O, then we would not take X either as a criterion or even as a sign or symptom of O.

6. What if B himself says that he is in pain? What is his criterion for saying that he is in pain? It is certain that he will not present his bodily behaviour as a criterion (of even as a sign or symptom) for his saying that he is in pain. Rather he experiences pain, and so he says that he is in pain.

But does not a serious difficulty threaten here? That is, if B's experience of pain is his criterion for saying that he is in pain, then, would his criterion not be a subjective one? But does the concept of a subjective criterion, a criterion which others are not able to make use of, not make sense? Must a criterion not be an objective criterion (does not the concept of a criterion involve the requirement of being an objective criterion)? Is it the case that just as a criterion must be a necessary one, as it seems, it must also be an objective one?

May it not be, as it looks, that the problem of a *criterion* is different from that of an *objective* criterion? May it not be, as it again looks, that there are criteria which are subjective (as in the case of B) and those which are objective, those which others are also able to make use of (as in the case of C in section 2)? And may it not even be, if I am permitted a little digression, that in some cases as that of B it is not at all possible to transcend a subjective criterion, however much that may be required from the point of scientific objectivity?

7. Can we understand a criterion in the sense of a paradigm case, in the sense of a particular but perfect, or more or less perfect, embodiment, or perfect, or more or less perfect, illustration, of a concept? That is, can we say that a criterion is not a generic term, as I have made it out to be in the preceding deliberations, but refers to just one specific kind of thing by which to identify an object (namely the kind of thing just-mentioned)? Thus, for example, we may say that a piece of granite is a criterion of a hard object, St. Francis is a criterion of a man of God, and the British House of Commons is a criterion of a parliament. Now, we can indeed take a paradigm case as a criterion of all other objects under that concept which it itself concretizes, albeit perfectly, or more or less perfectly. We can say that all these other objects are what they are by virtue of their conformity to the given paradigm case. But what is the criterion of a paradigm case itself? On what ground do we identify a paradigm case *as* a paradigm case? Must we not identify a paradigm case, and therefore ultimately all other objects as well which fall under a given concept, in those three ways which I have mentioned above? Must we not, for example, identify St. Francis as a perfect, or a more or less perfect, man of God by his conformity with the definition of a perfect man of God, or by his conformity with what logically follows from the definition of a perfect man of God, or by his possession of some attribute which is synthetically but necessarily connected with a perfect man of God?

8. Kant maintains that an action is moral if the maxim of that action can at the same time be willed as a universal law. Does this thesis provide the definition or a criterion of morality in Kant? When this question is asked, it is assumed that definition and criterion are two different things, such that X is either the definition or a criterion of an object. I have, on the other hand, tried to argue that criterion is a generic term of which definition is a species. This would mean that if Kant's thesis is

taken as a critertion of morality, then it must *be* either the definition of morality or one of those other two things which I have subsumed under criterion, and if it is taken as the definition of morality, then it must be a criterion of morality as well. But, one may ask here, is Kant's thesis a criterion in the sense of definition or in one of the other two senses of criterion? Now, is there any evidence in Kant to the effect that he did not understand a moral action *exactly* as an action the maxim of which can at the same time be willed as a universal law, that he did not take the term 'a moral action' and the term 'an action the maxim of which can at the same time be willed as a universal law' as *exactly* interchangeable terms? I for one find no such evidence. And if there is indeed no such evidence, then Kant's thesis would be a criterion in the sense of definition.

In brief, the question whether Kant's thesis provides a criterion or the definition of morality is based on the false view of criterion and definition being mutually exclusive terms. On the other hand, I have contended that definition is a species of criterion. And I have tried to show that Kant's thesis is a criterion in the sense of definition.

9. Suppose we say that there are objects which are characterized as ethical (good in themselves, independently of all other things), and that our knowledge of them is intuitive or through direct apprehension. But, then, is this knowledge, intuitive ethical knowledge, not open to the charge of being subjective (in the sense of being valid only for the person who claims to have this knowledge)? Or are there criteria by means of which this knowledge could be shown to be objective (in the sense of being valid for other persons as well)? Are there objective criteria of intuitive ethical knowledge?

Suppose, now, we say, as we must, that we have a direct or intuitive apprehension of a red patch in front of us. Is this intuitive physical knowledge also open to the charge of subjectivism? Or, are there objective criteria of this kind of knowledge?

Let us concede that under certain specified conditions, i.e. given a certain specified state of the world and a certain specified state of the body and mind, we all perceive that red patch in front of us. Could we, then, take these specified conditions as objective *criteria* of the given intuitive physical knowledge, i.e. as criteria by means of which not only I but others as well would know that red patch over there? But are these conditions not at best empirical, and not necessary? That is, are they not at best such that under them we all *do* in fact perceive that red patch over there, and not that under them we all *must* so perceive? And if so, how could we treat these conditions as objective *criteria,* as *necessary* grounds, of all of us knowing that red patch over there? How would we, on the basis of these conditions, come to terms with a person who did not perceive what others claimed to perceive? The extra-logical device of condemning this person as only fit for mental asylum would obviously not do.

Are there specified conditions under which we all perceive some ethical object, as there are presumably those under which we all perceive that red patch over there? But even if there were, they would not provide objective *criteria* of the given intuitive ethical knowledge, but at best only empirical conditions of all of us having that knowledge—just as in the former case.

10. Suppose, to take an example from Moore, we say that the object called 'Personal Affections' is intrinsically good. And suppose we accept Moore's following theses about this object: (1) that it consists of natural properties and the non-natural property of value, and (2) that although these two kinds of property are logically distinct, they are so related that a certain concatenation of natural properties necessarily has or is necessarily accompanied by the non-natural property of value, or that, in other words, they are so related that a certain concatenation of natural properties is necessarily but synthetically characterized by the non-natural property of value. What would here be the criterion of the object of 'Personal Affections' as being intrinsically good? What would be the ground of judging this object as so characterized? Evidently, firstly, the fact that this object is of that ethical nature which it is, the fact that it

possesses the non-natural property of value, and, secondly, the fact that it is that concatenation of natural properties which it is, the concatenation which is necessarily but synthetically related to the non-natural property of value. What other criterion could there be of the object under consideration? By what else could we identify it?

5

Kant's Definition of an Analytic Proposition – A Further Consideration

IN MY PAPER on 'Kant's Definition of an Analytic Proposition',[1] I have maintained that, in the IV portion of the Introduction of his *Critique of Pure Reason*[2], the portion entitled 'The Distinction between Analytic and Synthetic Judgements', Kant may be said to define an analytic judgement or proposition in four interchangeable ways. (1) An analytic proposition is one in which the predicate is already contained in the subject. (2) An analytic proposition is one in which the predicate is related to the subject through identity (undoubtedly in the sense of being partially or wholly identical with the subject). (3) An analytic proposition is one in which the predicate does not add anything to the subject but simply breaks it up or analyses it into its component parts. It is for this reason that Kant also calls an analytic proposition an explicative proposition. (4) An analytic proposition is one the denial of which would be self-contradictory.[3]

Now, in the beginning of the same portion of his *Critique of Pure Reason* from which I have taken the above-mentioned four interchangeable ways of defining an analytic proposition, Kant states that although in explaining the nature of the relation between the subject and the predicate of a proposition, that is, in explaining the nature of an analytic proposition as also a synthetic proposition, he has in mind only affirmative propositions of these two kinds, yet what he is saying with a view to these can be easily applied to negative propositions of these two kinds as well. And in the same portion he considers as an example of an affirmative analytic proposition the proposition 'All bodies are extended', and he considers as an example of an affirmative synthetic proposition the proposition 'All bodies are heavy'.

Now, it seems to me that there should be no difficulty in applying Kant's four interchangeable ways of defining an analytic proposition which I have mentioned in the preceding to affirmative analytic propositions. As a matter of fact, I have myself already applied them to an example of an affirmative analytic proposition in my aforementioned article, namely the example of the proposition 'A brother is a male'. I have explained there that, with respect to this proposition, we could say that in it the predicate concept of 'being a male' is already contained or included in, or is part and parcel of, the subject concept of 'being a brother'; the former is an element in the constitution of the latter. Or, we could say that in it 'being a male' is partially identical with 'being a brother', is identical with a part of the latter complex. Or we could say that in it 'being a male' does not add anything to 'being a brother', does not provide any new information about it, any information which is not already embodied in it, but simply makes explicit one of its (covert) constituents. Or, we could say that the denial of the predicate concept of 'being a male' to the subject concept of 'being a brother' would be self-contradictory. But although, as I have pointed out before, Kant himself does not see any difficulty in the matter, the question has been raised whether his various interchangeable ways of defining an analytic proposition can also be applied to negative analytic propositions, and if so, how.[4] This is the problem with which I wish to deal in the present paper.

In the latter part of his *Critique of Pure Reason* Kant makes suggestions about the application of some of the various ways in which I have found him to define an analytic proposition to negative analytic propositions. I would refer to these suggestions in due course.

2. Let me now take an example of a proposition which I consider to be an example of a negative analytic proposition, and then see whether Kant's four interchangeable ways of defining an analytic proposition which I have mentioned are applicable to it. I could take as an example of such a proposition 'A brother is not anything other than a male'. But for the sake of simplicity let me take a more specific version of this proposition, namely the proposition 'A brother is not a female'.

Now, to begin with, in respect of this proposition, could we say that in it the predicate concept of 'not being a female' is already contained or included in, or is part and parcel of, the subject concept of 'being a brother', that the former is already an element in the constitution of the latter? Or, to put it quite briefly and simply, could we say that in the given proposition the concept of 'not being a female' is already there within the meaning of 'being a brother'? We have seen that the concept of 'being a male' is already there within the meaning of 'being a brother'; 'being a brother' means, means at least, 'being a male'. But if this is so, then, it follows that the concept of 'not being anything other than a male' is also already there within the meaning of 'being a brother', and thus the concept of 'not being a female' is also already there within the meaning of 'being a brother'. One could express this thought generally by saying that if x is a constituent of a certain term, then, positively speaking, the concept of being x is already there within the content of being that term, and negatively speaking the concept of not being anything other than x, the concept of being not non-x, is also already there within the content of being that term; that is, every term has within its content any of its constituents and also the absence of the opposite of any of the given constituents. And thus, in respect of the proposition 'A brother is not a female', we could say that in it the concept of 'not being a female' is already contained in the concept of 'being a brother', just as much as, in respect of the proposition 'A brother is a male', we could say that in it the concept of 'being a male' is already contained in the concept of 'being a brother'.

Could we, now, say that, in the proposition 'A brother is not a female', the predicate concept of 'not being a female' is related to the subject concept of 'being a brother' by means of identity (undoubtedly in the sense of being partially or wholly identical with it), that, briefly and simply speaking, the concept of 'not being a female' is partially or wholly identical with the concept of 'being a brother'? We find that the reasoning involved in answering this question is exactly on the same lines as the reasoning involved in answering the previous question. And it is as follows. We have already seen that the concept of 'being a male' is partially identical with the concept of 'being a brother', is identical with a part of the latter complex. But if this is so, then it follows that the concept of 'not being a female' is also partially identical with the concept of 'being a brother', is identical with a part of the latter complex. One could express this thought generally by saying that if the concept of something called x is identical, partially or wholly, with a certain term, then, positively speaking, the concept of being x is identical, partially or wholly, with the concept of being that term, and negatively speaking, the concept of not being something other than x, the concept of being not non-x, is also identical, partially or wholly, with the concept of being that term; that is, every term is identical, partially or wholly, with any concept with which it is identical partially or wholly, and also identical, partially or wholly, with the concept of the absence of the opposite of that concept. And thus, in respect of the proposition 'A brother 'is not a female', we could say that in it the concept of 'not being a female' is partially identical with the concept of 'being a brother', just as much as, in respect of the proposition 'A brother is a male', we could say that in it the concept of 'being a male' is partially identical with the concept of 'being a brother'.

We may consider the following questions together: Could we say that, in the proposition 'A brother is not a female', the predicate concept of 'not being a female' does not add anything to the subject concept of 'being a brother', does not add any new information about it, any information which is not already embodied in it, but simply makes explicit or analyses some (covert) constituent or constituents of it? And, further, could we say that, in the given proposition, the denial of the predicate concept of 'not being a female' to the subject concept of 'being a brother' would be self-contradictory, or, quite briefly and simply, could we say that the proposition 'A brother is a female' is a self-contradictory proposition? Again, we find that the reasoning involved in answering these two questions is exactly on the same lines as the reasoning involved in answering the two earlier questions. Generally speaking, this line of reasoning is this: Given that the term S is related to the term P in a proposition in the manner m, then to find out what we can say both positively and negatively about the relationship of S and P in that proposition, and to see that, positively speaking, we can say that S is related to P in that proposition in the manner m, and negatively speaking, we can say that S is related to the term which is the negation of anything other than P, the term not non-P, in that proposition in the manner m, that is, to see that the term S is related to the term P in a proposition in that manner m in which it is related to it in that proposition, and it is also related to the term which signifies the absence of the opposite of P in that proposition in that same manner m. And thus, in the light of this general thesis, in respect of the proposition 'A brother is not a female', we could say that in it the predicate concept of 'not being a female' does not add anything to the subject concept of 'being a brother' but simply analyses or breaks up one of its component parts, just as much as, in respect of the proposition 'A brother is a male', we could say that in it the predicate concept of 'being a male' does not add anything to the subject concept of 'being a brother' but simply analyses or breaks up one of its component parts. And, further, in respect of the given proposition 'A brother is not a female', we could say that in it the denial of the predicate concept of 'not being a female' to the subject concept of 'being a brother' would be self-contradictory, just as much as, in respect of the proposition 'A brother is a male', we could say that in it the denial of the predicate concept of 'being a male' to the subject concept of 'being a brother' would be self-contradictory.

On page A 151 of his *Critique of Pure Reason,* Kant may be said to define a negative analytic proposition as one in which one can rightly deny in the predicate the opposite of what is already contained in the subject.[5] Thus, for example, if anyone maintains that 'A brother is a female', then one would be justified in denying feminity to a brother and maintaining that 'A brother is not a female'. Now, this definition is correct, but it will be seen that it is not expressed in strictly the same way in which the definition of an analytic proposition in general is expressed. In the fourth version of Kant's definition of an analytic proposition, which I have mentioned above and which is what is relevant here, it is said that an analytic proposition is one the denial of which would be self-contradictory. In the preceding I have tried to show that this definition is as much applicable to a negative analytic proposition as to an affirmative analytic proposition, as much to the proposition 'A brother is not a female' as to the proposition 'A brother is a male'.

On page A 154 of his *Critique of Pure Reason* Kant may be said to define an analytic proposition as one in which we take from the subject something which is already there in it and mention that thing in the predicate, an affirmative analytic proposition as one in which we say of the subject in the predicate what is already there in it, and a negative analytic proposition as one in which we say of the subject in the predicate that it is not the opposite of what is already there in it[6]. Thus, for example, on this definition of a negative analytic proposition, if the concept of 'being a male' is already there in the concept of 'being a brother', then the proposition 'A brother is not a female' would be a negative analytic proposition. Now, there is a sense in which the definition of a negative analytic proposition as mentioned here could be said to be correct, although in this sense its expression would not be in strict conformity with Kant's expression of his definition of an analytic proposition in general. Thus it could be said that the content of a concept has within it only what belongs to it positively and excludes from it anything which belongs to it negatively. But it seems to me that what belongs to a concept negatively is as much part and parcel of the content of that concept as what belongs to it positively. It seems to me, for example, that 'not being a female' is as much part and parcel of 'being a brother' as 'being a male'. In the preceding I have tried to show that Kant's third version of the definition of an analytic proposition, which is what is in view here and which I have also stated in the beginning of this paragraph, is as much applicable to a negative analytic proposition as to an affirmative analytic proposition, as much applicable to the proposition 'A brother is not a female' as to the proposition 'A brother is a male.'

Notes

1. *International Studies in Philosophy*, VIII. 1976.
2. Kant's *Critique of Pure Reason,* translated by Norman Kemp Smith, *Macmillan,* 1953 reprint.
3. Dharmendra Kumar has pointed out to me that those four ways of defining an analytic proposition which I have called interchangeable are not interchangeable. For, for example, whereas the first mode of definition could only apply to analytic proposition of the subject-predicate form, the fourth mode of definition would be applicable to analytic propositions of all forms.
   I am leaving Dharmendra Kumar's point mentioned here undiscussed for the time being.
4. This question has been raised by S. K. Bose in the course of a discussion on my paper on 'Kant's Definition of an Analytic Proposition' in a meeting of the Philosophical Society of St. Stephen's College, Delhi.
5. "... *If the judgement is analytic,* whether negative or affirmative, its truth can always be adequately known in accordance with the principle of contradiction. The reverse of that which as concept is

contained and is thought in the knowledge of the object, is always rightly denied.'

6. "In the analytic judgement we keep to the given concept, and seek to extract something from it. If it is to be affirmative, I ascribe to it only what is already thought in it. If it is to be negative, I exclude from it only its opposite."

6

Reasons in Ethics

ALL ETHICAL THEORIES, that is, theories which are aimed at giving what Kant calls the supreme principle of morality, the principle that ultimately determines whatever is to be called moral, may be classified under two heads.

(1) There are or may be ethical theories according to which the reason for a moral end being a moral end lies outside that end. That is, if the question is asked why one should bring into existence an end which is said to be a moral end, then the answer which is or may be given is that the realization of this end is a means to the realization of some end which is outside or other than it. Thus, in Mill, if the question is asked why one should bring justice into existence, then the answer which would be given is that the establishment of justice is conducive to the attainment of general happiness.

(2) There are or may be ethical theories according to which the reason for a moral end being a moral end does not lie outside that end but in that end itself. That is, if the question is asked why one should bring into existence an end which is said to be a moral end, then the answer which is or may be given is that it is itself the kind of end which it is said to be, and not that its realization is a means towards the realization of some end which is outside or other than it. Thus, in a philosopher like Moore, if the question is asked why one should bring justice into existence, then the answer which would be given is that it is

Ethical Theories

- 1. Heteronomous
  - 1.1 Heteronomous in the narrower sense
    - 1.11 Subjective or Psychological
      - 1.111 Explicitly
        - 1.1111 Extreme
        - 1.1112 Group
        - 1.1113 General
      - 1.112 Subjective in disguise
    - 1.12 Non-subjective or Non-Psychological
      - 1.121 Biological
      - 1.122 Non-biological, i.e., any non-subjective ethical theory other than biological
  - 1.2 Heteronomous in the wider sense
    - 1.21 Metaphysical
    - 1.22 Theological
    - 1.23 Any ethical theory which is heteronomous in the wider sense but which is other than metaphysical or theological
- 2. Autonomous
  - 2.1 Synthetic
  - 2.2 Analytic

itself that kind of end, and not that its establishment is conducive to the attainment of general happiness or something else.

I would here make use of the Kantian terminology, and call the former kind of ethical theory heteronomous ethical theory, and the latter kind of ethical theory autonomous ethical theory. And I would classify various actual or possible ethical theories under these two heads in the following way:

I have already defined a heteronomous ethical theory and an autonomous ethical theory.

1.1 An ethical theory which is heteronomous in the narrower sense is one according to which the reason for a moral end being a moral end lies in some fact of a natural science, like psychology or biology. Thus, for example, if one maintains that one ought to bring justice into existence, because some person or persons approve of the establishment of justice, or because the establishment of justice is conducive to the fulfilment of some basic human psychological and/or biological needs, then one would be having an ethical theory which is heteronomous in the narrower sense,

1.11 An ethical theory which is subjective or psychological is one according to which the reason for a moral end being a moral end lies in some fact of psychology, for instance that some person or persons approve of the establishment of justice. Now, in an ethical theory, a reference may be made to some fact of psychology explicitly, as when one maintains explicitly that one ought to establish justice because some person or persons approve of it; (1.111) or it may be made disguisedly, as when one thinks of a moral statement as no more than an emotive or exclamatory statement. (1.112) If the reference is to the state of mind of some one person, the speaker himself or some other, then we have an ethical theory which we may call extreme subjectivism. (1.1111) If the reference is to the state of mind of a group of persons, like some particular social group, then we have an ethical theory which we may call group subjectivism, which is nothing other than a sociological ethical theory. (1.1112) If the reference is to the state of mind of the whole or most of mankind, as in Hume, then we have an ethical theory which we may call general subjectivism.

1.12 An ethical theory which is non-subjective or non-psychological is one according to which the reason for a moral end being a moral end lies in some fact of some natural science other than psychology, for instance that there are some basic human biological needs. If the fact referred to is a fact of biology, then we have an ethical theory which we may call a biological ethical theory. (1.121) If the fact referred to is a fact of some natural science other than biology (and, of course, other than psychology), then we have an ethical theory which we may call a non-biological ethical theory. (1.122) I am not aware of the actual existence of any ethical theory which is heteronomous in the narrower sense and which is neither psychological in my sense of that term, nor biological . But there might be an ethical theory of that sort some time, say, an ethical theory in which a reference is made to some fact of physics.

1.2 An ethical theory which is heteronomous in the wider sense is one, according to which the reason for a moral end being a moral end lies in some fact of some study other than a natural science, like metaphysics or theology. Thus, for example, if one maintains that one ought to bring justice into existence, because God commands or wills it, then one would be having an ethical theory which is heteronomous in the wider sense. If, in an ethical theory, the reason which is given for a moral end being a moral end lies in some fact of metaphysics, like the Nature of the Stoics, then we have a metaphysical ethical theory. (1 .21) If this reason lies in some fact of theology, like a divine commandment, then we have a theological ethical theory. (1.22) And if this reason lies in some fact of some study other than metaphysics or theology (and, of course, other than a natural science), like logic as in the case of Clarke and Cudworth, or aesthetics as in the case of Shaftesbury and Hutcheson, then we would have an ethical theory which is heteronomous in the wider sense and which is other than metaphysical or theological (1.123).

2.1 An autonomous ethical theory which is synthetic is one according to which the reason for a moral end being a moral end is provided by what may be called the real or synthetic definition of a moral end *qua* a moral end, that is, by a definition which brings to light the reality to which a moral end *qua a* moral end refers, as in Moore.

2.2 An autonomous ethical theory which is analytic is one according to which the reason for a moral end being a moral end is provided by what may be called the verbal or analytic definition of a moral end *qua* a moral end, that is, by a definition which does no more than refer to the content itself of the concept of a moral end *qua* a moral end, as in Kant on one particular interpretation. (In my paper on 'Does Kant commit the Naturalistic Fallacy?' included in the *Akten des IV Internationalen Kant-Kongresses (de Gruyter & Co.* 1974), also later included in my book, *Towards Purity of Morals*, (Pragati Publications, 1993), I have worked out this particular interpretation.)

Now, all heteronomous ethical theories are open to the following insuperable difficulty. Whenever somebody maintains that the reason for a moral end being a moral end lies outside it, that the reason for a moral end being a moral end is some further end, then the question may be asked whether this further end itself is a moral end or a non-moral end. If it is a non-moral end, then it cannot account for a moral end being a moral end:- to suppose that it can would be to commit what Moore called the naturalistic fallacy. If it is a moral end, then the question would arise about the reason for this further moral end being a moral end. As a result of following this query, one would easily see that a heteronomous ethical theory would either be involved in committing the naturalistic fallacy or in infinite regress.

As far as autonomous ethical theories which are analytic, in the sense in which Kant's ethical theory is analytic on one particular interpretation of that theory, are concerned, they do not really provide us with any reason for a moral end being a moral end. They simply give us analytic propositions, which may be tautologies or other than tautologies, propositions like 'A moral end, which is a universally valid end, is a universally valid end.' As far as autonomous ethical theories which are synthetic are concerned, they are evidently not trivial like autonomous ethical theories which are analytic. They are also not exposed to the difficulty to which heteronomous ethical theories are exposed. They do not involve the commission of the naturalistic fallacy, because they do not account for a moral end being a moral end by means of some non-moral end. And they do not involve infinite regress, because they do not involve a reference to the reason for a moral end being a moral end further and further on. But autonomous ethical theories which are synthetic are exposed to some other difficulty, although, if I may say so in passing, this difficulty does not seem to me to be peculiar to these. The difficulty is this. Suppose someone asks, how does one know that the reason for a moral end being a moral end lies in that end itself or how does one know that that end itself is a moral end? Then, all that one can say in answer to this question is that one knows it directly or immediately, that, in other words, one intuits it. And, of course, as soon as one says that one is bound to be confronted with the charge of subjectivism like a bad dream, the charge that what one person or set of persons intuits as a moral end another person or set of persons may not do.

The conclusions which we can draw from the above deliberations are as follows: (1) we cannot look for the reason for a moral end being a moral end in a non-moral end. To do so would be illogical, would involve the naturalistic fallacy, (2) If we look, or ultimately look, for the reason for a moral end being a moral end in that end itself then we are exposed to the danger of subjectivism. As a result, in respect of looking for reasons in ethics we find ourselves faced with the dilemma of either being illogical or being subjectivistic. This brings to light some of our ignorance, some of what would seem to be our irremediable ignorance, in the field of ethics.

7

Analytic and Synthetic Propositions

1. ALTHOUGH I HAVE written this paper as an independent paper, I would like to preface it by saying that it is really in response to some of the things which have been said in the context of analytic and synthetic propositions.

(1) In recent times, as far as I know, Kant's definition of an analytic proposition as one in which the subject contains the predicate (and his definition of a synthetic proposition as one in which this is not so) has been criticized on two grounds. Firstly, it has been said that this definition is at best applicable to propositions of the subject-predicate form. And secondly, it has been said that as making use of the notion of containment, it is metaphorical in character. Now, without for the time being going into the merit of these criticisms, I would like to say that there is in Kant yet another definition of an analytic proposition (and yet another definition of a synthetic proposition) which is clearly not exposed to these criticisms; and in the course of this paper I have maintained that one can indeed define an analytic proposition by means of this definition (and a synthetic proposition by means of its this other definition), namely that an analytic proposition is one the denial of which would be self-contradictory (and a synthetic proposition is one the denial of which would not be self-contradictory). (2) Kant also defines an analytic proposition as one in which the predicate simply analyses or explicates the subject into its component parts (and a synthetic

proposition as one in which the predicate adds something to the subject). For this reason Kant calls an analytic proposition an explicative proposition (and a synthetic proposition an ampliative proposition). Now, I find that a very large number of examples of analytic propositions which are mentioned, including Kant's own famous example 'All bodies are extended' and other examples like 'A bachelor is an unmarried person' and 'A brother is a male sibling', are really not of an explicative, but of a more or less reiterative kind. And I find that analytic propositions which are of an explicative kind are those which we obtain on the basis of logical or conceptual analysis, like those which we obtain on the basis of Russell's Theory of Description. (3) Further, Kant defines an analytic proposition as one in which the predicate is related to the subject through identity (and a synthetic proposition as one in which the predicate is related to the subject without identity). Now, I find this to be a matter of very great interest that there are identical propositions which are not analytic, the most striking of these being those in which an empirically given class of objects is defined *per genus et differentiam*, propositions like 'Man is a rational animal' or 'Man is a being in whom existence precedes essence'. Although these are identical propositions, yet they are synthetic propositions and are no more than of the nature of hypotheses.[1]

So much by way of a historical prefatory note to the following reflections.

2. One may call the proposition 'A brother is a brother', in its literal meaning, straightway as an analytic proposition. One may also call the proposition 'A brother is a male sibling' as an analytic proposition, on the assumption that in this proposition the expression 'a brother' means the same thing as the expression 'a male sibling'. That is, one may also call the proposition 'A brother (male sibling) is a male sibling' straightway as an analytic proposition. If in the proposition A brother is a male sibling', the expression 'a brother' did not mean the same thing as the expression 'a male sibling' but meant what, say, the expression 'a fellow member of a religious order' meant, then this

proposition would not only be not analytic, it could even be false. Further, one may also call the propositions 'A brother (male sibling) is a male' and 'A brother (male sibling) is a sibling' straightway as analytic propositions.

One may call the proposition 'A brother is a brother', in its literal meaning, and 'A brother (male sibling) is a male sibling' as analytic propositions which are tautologies. And one may call the propositions 'A brother (male sibling) is a male' and 'A brother (mile sibling) is a sibling' as analytic propositions which are not tautologies. One may define an analytic proposition which is a tautology as an analytic proposition which can be shown to consist of terms which are exactly coincident with one another, or as an analytic proposition which can be shown to be an exactly identical proposition. And one may define an analytic proposition which is not a tautology as an analytic proposition which can be shown to consist of terms which are not exactly coincident with one another, or as an analytic proposition which can be shown to be not an exactly identical proposition.

And, following Kant, one may define an analytic proposition as one the denial of which would be self-contradictory.

3. Now, take the proposition 'I know that p' (where 'p' stands for a particular proposition). And suppose that, on the basis of the analysis of the concept of knowledge as contained in this proposition, we find that this proposition is equivalent to the propositions (1) I believe that p, (2) p (or p is true), and (3) I have evidence for believing that p. Then one may call the proposition 'If I know that p, then (1) I believe that p, (2) p, and (3) I have evidence for believing that p' as an analytic proposition (which presumably is a tautology), on the ground that its denial would be self-contradictory, on the ground that one could not logically maintain that one knew that p and at the same time deny (1) that one believed that p and/or (2) that p and/or (3) that one had evidence for believing that p.

I have said that we obtain the proposition 'If I know that p, then (1) I believe that p, (2) p, and (3) I have evidence for believing that p' on the basis of the analysis of the concept of knowledge as contained in the proposition 'I know that p'. We do not, cannot (ultimately) obtain it in the way in which we obtain the proposition 'A brother is a male sibling' (if x is a brother, then x is a male sibling'). All that we need to do, in order to obtain this latter proposition, is to consult a dictionary and see what meaning or meanings the expression 'brother' has there or to consult the usage or usages from which a dictionary is compiled. This relatively easy device is not available to us for obtaining the former proposition; no amount of consulting a dictionary or usages from which a dictionary is compiled would help here. What we need to do here is to take up 'I know that p' (or one or more of its concrete forms like 'I know that, in a large state, an individual is constantly becoming like a part of a machine', 'I know that Ethics has simply to choose between Intuitionism and Naturalism or Heteronomy), and reflect upon or think about the content of the concept of knowledge as contained in this proposition. This reflection or thinking may consist, for example, in distinguishing the proposition from other propositions with which it may be confused (propositions like 'I believe that *p*,' I believe that p and p is true') and concentrating upon the concept of knowledge as contained in it to see what are the various elements which compose it, what all is involved in its constitution. I do not wish to say here that the content of the concept of knowledge as contained in the proposition 'I know that p' which we find to belong to it through the just-mentioned ways does not belong to it in exactly the same sense as the content 'male sibling' belongs to the concept of brother, to one particular concept as embodied in the expression 'brother'. However, what we find to be the case is that, unlike with proposition 'A brother (male sibling) is a male sibling', the content here is entirely implicit and has to be made explicit or brought to light in the ways just-mentioned.

4. Now, on the basis of what I have said in the preceding two sections, one may classify analytic propositions as follows:

- Analytic Propositions
  - 1. Straightforwardly Reiterative
    - 1. 1.Reiterative of the whole of the given term in the proposition concerned (e.g., 'A brother is a brother', 'A brother (male sibling) is a male sibling)
    - 1.2 Reiterative of a part of the given term in the proposition concerned (e.g., 'A brother (male sibling) is a male')
  - 2. Explicative
    - 2.1 Explicative of the whole of the given term in the proposition concerned (e.g., 'If I know that p, then (1) I believe that p, (2) p, and (3) I have evidence for believing that p').
    - 2.2. Explicative of a part of the given term in the proposition concerned (e.g., 'If I know that p, then I believe that p')

Here both 1.1, that is, analytic proposition in which there is a straightforward reiteration of the whole of the given term, and 2.1, that is analytic propositions in which there is an explication of the whole of the given term, would be tautologies.

One may take '(a + b) is (a + b)/(a/b)' as the standard form of all analytic propositions, both straightforwardly reiterative and explicative, and both those which are tautologies and those which are not tautologies.

5. Following Kant once more, one may define a synthetic proposition as one the denial of which would not be self-contradictory.

Now, let me take an empirically given class, like the class of human beings, consisting of members ABCD and symbolize this class as X and another class, like the class of animals, consisting of members EFGH and symbolize this class as Y. And let me suppose that there is a certain characteristic, c1, which the members of the class X possess and which they share with the members of the class Y, a characteristic which is common to the members of both the class X and the class Y, and that there is a certain characteristic, c2, which the members of the class X also possess but which they do not share with the members of the class Y, a characteristic which is peculiar to them, to the members of the class X. Then, following Aristotle's thesis about the nature of definition as *per genus et differentiam,* one may say that the characteristics c1 and c2 constitute the definition, are the defining characteristics, of the class X, that the statement 'X is c1 c2' is a statement of the definition of X by means of c1 and c2.

Now, as regards the statement or proposition 'X is c1 c2', although as a definition it is an identical proposition in which the term defined 'X' (*definiendum*) and the defining term 'c1 c2' (*definiens*) are interchangeable with one another, one may say that it is a synthetic, not an analytic, proposition, because its denial would not be self-contradictory. That is, although, as it is or as a matter of fact, the class X has the characteristics cl and c2 as its defining characteristics, it *could* have some other characteristics, say the characteristics cl and c3 or c3 and c4 as its defining characteristics. This would seem to me to be a rather interesting phenomenon, because it will show that the class of identical propositions is wider than the class of tautologies (and the class of partially identical propositions wider than the class of partially identical analytic propositions), that there could be identical propositions which are not analytic.

6. I have said that the characteristics c1 and c2 are the defining characteristics of the class X. Now, the class X could also have other characteristics, say, the characteristics c5 and c6 which are not included among its defining characteristics, and as a result which we may simply call its non-defining characteristics. Now, I prefer to call c1 and c2 as the defining, and c5 and c6 as the non- defining, characteristics of the class X, to calling the former essential and the latter accidental characteristics of the class X. For the expression 'essential', as distinguished from the expression 'accidental' could lead one to believe that the chracteristics which are called essential characteristics, the characteristics c1 and c2, *must* belong to the class to which they are said to belong, to the class X, such that the class would simply cease to be that class unless it had those chaiacteristics. On the other hand, according to my own contention, both the sets of characteristics, the set of defining characteristics c1 and c2 and the set of non-defining characteristics c5 and c6 are such that they just *do*, just *happen,* to belong to the class X, such that neither of them need have belonged to the class X. They differ from one another only in the way in which they are found to belong to the class X, and consequently in the way in which they delimit the class X (from, say, the class Y). The characteristics cl and c2 belong to all the members of the class X, and belong only to these; the characteristics c5 and c6, although they may belong to all these, do not belong only to these. And consequently the characteristics c1 and c2 delimit the class X (from, say, the class Y) with a finality with which the characteristics c5 and c6 do not and cannot do.

Now, even if there should be a controversy about whether or not the proposition 'X is c1 and c2' is a synthetic proposition, that is, is a proposition the denial of which would not be self-centradictory, there will be no controversy about the proposition 'X is c5 c6' as being a proposition the denial of which would not be self-contradictory. As a result, we already obtain the following two kinds of synthetic propositions: (1) general propositions which embody the definition, the defining characteristics obtained *per genus et differentiam,* of an empirically given class of objects; and (2) general propositions which embody a characteristic or characteristics of an empirically given class of objects other than the defining characteristics of that class obtained *per genus et differentiam*—in brief, we might say, (1) general propositions which embody the defining characteristics of an empirically given class of objects; and (2) general propositions which embody the non-defining characteristics of an empirically given class of objects.

One may take 'X is c' (where 'X' stands for an empirically given class of objects, and 'c' for a defining characteristic or characteristics obtained *per genus et differentiam,* or a non-defining characteristic or characteristics of 'X') as the standard form of the above mentioned two kinds of synthetic proposition.

7. There are what I consider to be other interesting cases of synthetic propositions, besides the one of 'general propositions which embody the definition, the defining characteristics, obtained *per genus et differentiam,* of an empirically given class of objects', which I have mentioned above, although these other cases are perhaps not quite as interesting as this one. I include among these other cases the following: (1) propositions in which the object referred to is the same although different things are said of it, that is, in which there is identity of denotation but difference in connotation ('The person who is going away as a Visiting Professor is the same who accused Abdul the other day'), and (2) propositions in which the object referred to is the same but different names are used for it, that is, in which there is the identity of denotation but difference in designations ('Vivek is the same person as Kaku'). Both these kinds of proposition, although they are also identical propositions in a way, are synthetic propositions, because their denial would not be self-contradictory. However, it is not a part of my present purpose to

make an exhaustive list of these synthetic propositions and also those other than these. What I wish to do for the time being is just the following.

I have said above that the obtaining of an analytic proposition which is straightforwardly reiterative is a relatively easy, indeed, one might even say, a rather simple matter. All that we need to do, in order to obtain it, is (1) to take a concept (for example, the concept of a brother), the content of which is already known to us quite explicitly through a dictionary or the usages from which a dictionary is compiled (for example, the concept of a brother as the concept of a male sibling), and (2) to simply assert this concept of itself, either in respect of the whole of its content or in respect of a part of its content (for example, 'A brother is a male sibling', 'A brother is a male', 'A brother is a sibling'). But as far as the obtaining of an analytic proposition which is explicative is concerned, it is as difficult a matter as any in Philosophy. (The obtaining of this, I think, is also admittedly at least one major task of Philosophy.)

We may, for example, take the concept of 'knowledge' as embodied in the proposition 'I know that p', or the concept of 'ought' as embodied in the proposition 'One ought to bring the object X into existence unconditionally', for analysis. And we would find that it may take us any amount of time and require any amount of effort on our part towards obtaining even a partial analysis, towards determining even a partial content, of these concepts. How long did it take us and what efforts did it cause us to obtain, through some methods as I have mentioned above, the analysis of the proposition 'I know that p' into '(1) I believe that p, (2) p, and (3) I have evidence for believing that p'? And are we quite sure even now that we have after all struck the exact and full, or more or less full, content of this proposition? And how long is it taking us and what efforts is it causing us to obtain, again through the same sort of methods indicated in respect of the other case, the exact and full, or more or less full, content of the concept of 'ought' as embodied in the proposition 'One ought to bring the object X into existence unconditionally', the exact and full, or more or less full, analysis of the proposition 'One *ought* to bring the object X into existence unconditionally?' I think that I am not wrong in saying that we are still groping, we are still at loggerheads with one another.

Note

1. In my paper, 'Kant's Definition of an Analytic Proposition', *International Studies in Philosophy,* VIII. 1976, I have dealt with the two recently made criticisms of Kant's definition of an analytic proposition as one in which the subject contains the predicate; and also brought to light four definitions of an analytic proposition (and correspondingly four definitions of a synthetic proposition) which one may discover in Kant and which I have mentioned here, and then talked about the relationship among these definitions. This paper is also included in this book under the title 'Kant's Definition of an Analytic Proposition'.

8

Phenomenalism, Idealism and Mentalism: A Historical Note

1. ONE MAY BE said to be a phenomenalist of one form or another depending upon what he means by the term phenomenon. Let me mention here just three senses in which this term has been understood in the history of philosophy. (1) There is the sense of this term in which it means a direct or indirect object of sense-experience, like, generally speaking, the ideas or perceptions of the British empiricists. (2) There is the sense of this term in which it means an appearance as distinguished from reality, like the world of sensible particulars in the case of Plato or the world of nature (the world of knowledge) in the case of Kant. (3) There is the sense of this term in which it means an object (which happens to be an essence or meaning or universal) given in our transcendental consciousness through some form of intuition, like the Ideas of Husserl.[1] Thus we may say that, for example, Hume is a phenomenalist in respect of ideas or perceptions which he takes to be constitutive of the material world and the self; Plato and Kant are phenomenalists in respect of the world of sensible particulars and the world of nature, respectively, as being appearances of something real; and Husserl is a phenomenalist (he calls himself a phenomenologist) in

1. I am extremely grateful to now the late S. K. Bose for his detailed comments on an ealier draft of this paper.

respect of Ideas which he considers as things themselves. Hence if somebody raises the question whether such and such a person is a phenomenalist, the question which would have to be first answered is, phenomenalist in what sense?

2. Idealism is the exact opposite of Realism.Both of them are theories, possibly among other things, about the metaphysical and epistemological relation of the mind to the world. According to Realism, (1) the world exists and has the nature which it has independently of the mind, and (2) the world can be known as it is in itself directly or indirectly. One may call the first part of Realism, the part dealing with how things are, Metaphysical Realism, and the second part, the part dealing with what we can know, Epistemological Realism. According to Idealism, (1) the world does not exist and does not have the nature which it has independently of the mind, but only as being dependent upon it, and (2) the world is not or cannot be known as it is in itself, but only as being given through some subjective ways, empirical or *a priori*. Correspondingly one may call the first part of Idealism, Metaphysical Idealism and the second part, Epistemological Idealism.

It is possible for a philosopher, as in the case of Kant, to be a Metaphysical Realist and an Epistemological Idealist.

I have just said that, according to Metaphysical Idealism, the world depends upon the mind for its existence and nature. But we find that philosophers may differ from one another about what *part* of the mind they make the existence and nature of the world dependent upon. Thus, Hume would make the existence and nature of the world (in his case the self and the material world) dependent upon *sensible* ideas or perceptions, Hegel on the *rational* part of the mind, and Schopenhauer on the *volitional* part. This fact would enable us to distinguish between different forms of Metaphysical Idealism; and it would be in the fitness of things to invent specific names for these different forms, although I am not in a position to do so at present. Let me mention here in passing, even though it is not material to my interest in this place, that we find that philosophers may differ from one another not merely about what *part* but also, for

A Classification of Idealistic Theories

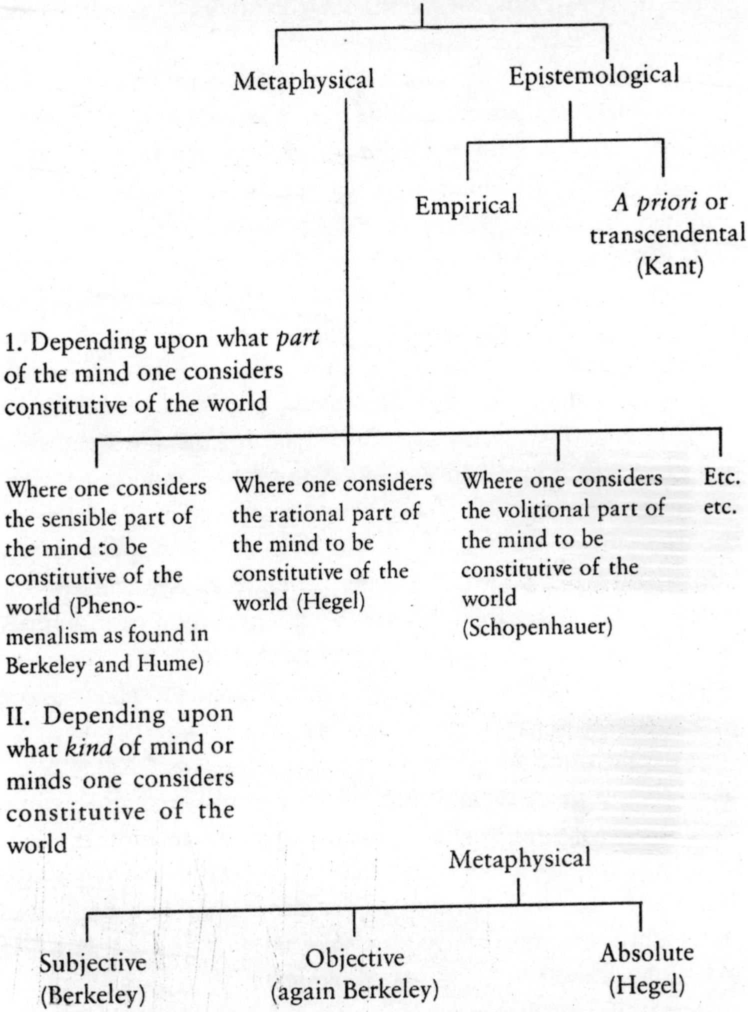

example, what *kind* of mind or minds they make the existence and nature of the world dependent upon. In this latter sort of case it is, that we have such forms of Metaphysical Idealism as Subjective Idealism (Berkeley), Objective Idealism (again Berkeley) and Absolute Idealism (Hegel).

It will be seen from the above that Phenomenalism of that particular variety which we find, say, in Hume, the variety according to which phenomena are sensible ideas or perceptions which are constitutive of the material world and the self, would be a form of Metaphysical Idealism.

3. Two of the things which I have tried to say in the preceding deliberations are as follows: (1) Phenomenalism is not a name of just one kind of theory but of different kinds of theories, and (2) Phenomenalism of that particular variety which we find, say, in Hume is a form of Metaphysical Idealism. Now, there is one more thing which I would like to say here. And it is as follows. As we have seen above, Idealism and Realism are theories, possibly among other things, about the metaphysical and epistemological relation of the mind to the world. As distinguished from these, (a) Materialism, whether (i) Mechanistic or Reductive (Hobbes) or (ii) Dialectical (Marx and Engels) or (iii) Emergent (Lloyd Morgan and Samuel Alexander), (b) Mentalism (Leibniz) and (c) Neutralism (Russell), among others, are theories about what kind of material or stuff the world is ultimately made of, what are the ultimate constituents of the world. Now, we notice a remarkable phenomenon here, namely that although Idealism and Mentalism are theories about two different questions altogether, Idealism (Metaphysical) turns out to be Mentalism. For, in maintaining that the nature and existence of the world are dependent upon the mind, Idealism, just like Mentalism, is maintaining that the world is mental. Thus, for example, Hume's sensible ideas or perceptions are as much of mental entities as Leibniz's monads, however much in all the other ways they may differ from one another. So this is the third thing which I wish to say in this place, namely this that Idealism (Metaphysical) is found to be Mentalism.

4. I have no desire to confuse the question, among other things. about the metaphysical and epistemological relation of the mind to the world with the question about the material or stuff the world is ultimately made of, nor the alternative answers to the former question with the alternative answers to the latter question.

What I wish to say is this: if one is an idealist (metaphysical) in answer to the former question, then he *must* be a mentalist in answer to the latter question, whether or not he explicitly deals with this question. This is simply a logical corollary. For, as I have just pointed out above, however much in all the other ways sensible ideas or perceptions of Hume and monads of Leibniz may differ from one another, they are both undoubtedly mental.

Similarly there is this other logical corollary: if one is a materialist, whether reductive or dialectical or emergent, in answer to the latter question, then he *must* be a realist (at least metaphysical) in answer to the former question, whether or not he explicitly deals with this question. For in that case, according to him, the material conditions of which the mind is a product or emergent must already be there as being or existing independently of the mind.

Generally speaking, the following would be an interesting although a long and possibly arduous exercise to do: Take various alternative answers to one philosophical question and various alternative answers to another philosophical question, and then see what, if any, are the logical relations among these. Let me illustrate this point by one or two more examples. If one is a mechanistic or reductive materialist in answer to the question about the material or stuff which the world is ultimately made of, then he *must* quite obviously be a determinist in answer to the question 'Is there Free Will?', whether or not he explicitly deals with this question, And likewise, if one is an empiricist, say, in the sense of Hume, in answer to the question 'What is the origin or source of knowledge?', then he cannot be a realist like Plato or Aristotle or even a conceptualist like Locke but *must* be a nominalist like Berkeley or something of that sort in answer to the question 'What are Universals?', whether or not he explicitly deals with this question. For, as Plato contended in his *Theaetetus,* sense-experience pure and simple cannot be the source of our knowledge of anything which is more than a particular.

9

Public and Private Use of Reason

Part One

According to Kant, in his essay on "An Answer to the Question: 'What is Enlightenment'," [1] (*i*) a person is immature, if he is unable to use his own understanding without the guidance of others; (*ii*) a person has self-incurred immaturity, if, although he has understanding, he does not have the resolution and courage to use it without the guidance of others; and (*iii*) a person is enlightened, if he has emerged out of his self-incurred immaturity, that is, if he has acquired the resolution and courage to use his own understanding without the guidance of others.[2]

Kant distinguishes between public and private use of reason. He defines the former as a person's addressing the entire reading public, in virtue of his being a man of leaning. And he defines the latter as a person's obeying the dictates of the position which he may be occupying in a certain social set-up, be that civil life, army, or church. According to him, a person is obliged to obey the dictates of the position which he may be occupying in a certain social set-up in the interest of that set-up. And he should be allowed to address the entire reading public in all matters in virtue of his being a member of society in general, as well as a man of learning in the interest of truth. "Now in some affairs which affect the interests of the commonwealth, we require a certain mechanism whereby some members of the commonwealth must behave purely passively, so that they may, by an artificial common agreement, be employed by the government for public ends (or at least deterred from vitiating them). It is, of course, impermissible to argue in such cases. Obedience is imperative. But in so far as this or that individual who acts as part of the machine also considers himself as a member of a complete commonwealth or even of cosmopolitan society, and thence as a man of learning who may through his writings address a public in the truest sense of the word, he may indeed argue without harming the affairs in which he is employed for some of the time in a passive capacity. Thus it would be very harmful if an officer receiving an order from his superiors were to quibble openly, while on duty, about the appropriateness or usefulness of the order in question. He must simply obey. But he cannot reasonably be banned from making observations as a man of learning on the errors in the military service, and from submitting these to the public for judgement. The citizen cannot refuse to pay the taxes imposed upon him. Presumptuous criticisms of such taxes, where someone is called upon to pay them, may be punished as an outrage which could lead to general insubordination. Nonetheless, the same citizen does not contravene his civil obligations, if, as a learned individual, he publicly voices his thoughts on the impropriety or even injustice of such fiscal measures. In the same way, a clergyman is bound to instruct his pupils and his congregation in accordance with the doctrines of the church he serves; for, he was employed by it on that condition. But as a scholar, he is completely free as well as obliged to impart to the public all his carefully considered, well-intentioned thoughts on the mistaken aspects of those doctrines, and to offer suggestions for a better arrangement of religious and ecclesiastical affairs. And there is nothing in this which need trouble the conscience. For what he teaches in pursuit of his duties as an active servant of the church is presented by him as something which he is not empowered to teach at his own discretion, but which he is employed to expound in a prescribed manner and in someone else's name. He will say: "Our church teaches this or that, and these are the arguments it uses." He then extracts as much practical value as possible for his congregation from precepts to which he would not himself prescribe with full conviction, but which he can nevertheless undertake to expound, since it is not wholly impossible that they may contain truth. At all events, nothing opposed to the essence of religion is present in such doctrines. For, if the clergyman thought he could find anything of this sort in them, he would not be able to carry out his official duties in good conscience, and would have to resign. Thus the use which someone employed as a teacher makes of his reason in the presence of his congregation is purely private, since a congregation, however large it is, is never any more than a domestic gathering. In view of this, he is not and cannot be free as a priest, since he is acting on a commission imposed from outside. Conversely, as a scholar addressing the real public (i.e. the world at large) through his writings, the clergyman making public use of reason enjoys unlimited freedom to use his own reason and to speak in his own person."[3]

According to Kant, the public becomes enlightened through the public use of reason.

I would like to ask the question: is Kant justified in maintaining that a person who occupies a certain position in a certain social set-up, while being obliged to obey the dictates of his position in that set-up in the interest of that set-up, should be completely free, as a member of society in general and as a man of learning, to address the entire public in all matters in the interest of truth? I am not presently asking the question whether this person is obliged to obey the dictates of his position under all conditions; I reserve this question for Part Two of this paper.

Let me take an example. Person A is a member of a certain academic set-up. Members, say, of a particular denomination, who are admitted to that set-up, do not have to fulfil the same requirements as the members of other denominations. The reason given is that the members of that particular denomination have long been handicapped somehow, and therefore they are not always able to fulfil the same requirements as the members of other denominations, and hence it is only fair that they are given some preferential treatment enabling them to catch up with the rest.

Let me take another example which is continued from the first. The given academic set-up, which one may call S_1 is under an obligation to follow the basic principles of a certain social set-up, which one may call S_2. The person A, who is a member of S_1 and also of S_2, finds that the preferential treatment which S_1 accords to the members of the just-mentioned denomination is in conflict with the basic principle of non-discrimination which S_2 professes and has undertaken to uphold. He brings it to the notice of S_2 and appeals to it to do something in the matter. However, S_2 vindicates S_1 and considers it fair that the people who have long been handicapped are given preferential treatment enabling them to catch up with the rest.

Kant's contention, as we have seen, is that, as a member of S_1 A is obliged to support S_1's giving preferential treatment to the members of the denomination concerned, and the ground on which it does so. And he is obliged to do this in the interest of S_1. Likewise, as a member of S_2, A is obliged to go along with S_2's vindication of S_1, and the ground on which it does so which is the same as before. And he is obliged to do this in the interest of S_2. But, while this is the case, as a member of society in general and as a man of learning, A should be allowed, by S_1 and S_2 as well, to address the entire public about, to discuss before the entire public, what S_1 does and what S_2 does. And he should be allowed to do this in the interest of truth, in the interest of getting at the right thing. Thus A may argue, as against what both S_1 and S_2 are doing, that it is unfortunate that the members of the denomination concerned have been handicapped, that as a result it is true that they are not always able to fulfil the same requirements as the members of other denominations, but that giving them preferential treatment is not the best thing to do. For, in the first place, it is most likely that it will put them in a state of mind where they think that they have already caught up with the rest and this will have the corollary that S_1 and S_2 will suffer, amongst other things, in terms of quality. And, in the second place, it is most likely that once the preferential treatment is there, they will want it to be perpetuated towards an easy fulfilment of their own self-interest. A may go on to appeal for the evolution of an alternative course of action. He may say that, whatever may ultimately emerge to be the concrete shape of this course of action, it has to have the ingredient that no one will have a position which he is not fit to handle, and as a consequence it has to have the ingredient that one would do one's best to equip the members of the denomination concerned to compete with the rest for any position which there may be. A may further admit that it will be far from easy to evolve such a course of action.

My question is: is Kant justified in maintaining that the person A, while being obliged to obey the dictates of his position in S_1 and S_2 in the interest of S_1 and S_2, should be completely free, as a member of society in general and as a man of learning to address the entire public in all matters in the interest of truth? Now, this question is easily answered. It goes without saying that the person A does not only belong to S_1 and S_2 in the way in which he does so, he is also a member of human society in general, is also one of mankind. It is also possible that, while being bound by what is demanded of him by virtue of his position in S_1 and S_2, he is of the view that what is so demanded of him is not quite the right thing, is not quite the truth; and therefore, in the interest of what is the right thing, he would like to present his point of view for discussion before the people at large as a forum for this purpose. Thus it is evident that, in the interest of what is the right thing, he should be allowed to do what he intends doing. One may add here, although it is not relevant for the present argument, that, from the point of what is the right thing, humanity would only be better off by his being allowed to do what he intends doing. Hence, to revert to the argument, Kant is right in advocating the public use of reason.

Now, although this is so, there could be another point of view in the matter. There could be the point of view that the public use of reason should not be allowed (there is at least a serious frowning upon the public use of reason). On the basis of this approach, it is maintained that a person who occupies a certain position in a certain social set-up is obliged to obey the dictates of that position, and that is that. There may be but need not be, in that set-up, forums where the person can give expression to what he thinks. But after that has been done and the forums mentioned have done all that they thought fit to do, there is nothing more to do. The reason which is given in support of this contention is twofold. Firstly, the world at large would otherwise think that there is something not quite all right in the given set-up, that there is tension and infighting there, and that would sully the image of unity (or shall we say, unanimity) of that set-up and expose it to public disrepute. And, secondly, the public use of reason is a challenge to the authorities in that set-up. In brief, one may say that there could be another point of view in the matter, according to which it is in the interest of a given social set-up both that a person who occupies a certain position in that set-up is obliged to obey the dictates of that position and that he is not allowed the public use of reason; and further, the public use of reason is a challenge to the authorities in that set-up (which may also be said to be against the interest of that set-up).

Now, as far as the first reason is concerned, on the basis of the other point of view, it is not denied that a person who occupies a certain position in a certain social set-up is a member of human society in general as well. It is also not denied that there may be, in addition, other interests than the interest of the given set-up, say, the interest of truth or the interest of humanity at large. However, what is affirmed, at least implicitly, is that the interest of the given set-up holds sway over all other interests (we could say, normally speaking). Now, it is not clear why, according to this other point of view, the interest of the given set-up holds sway over all other interests. It is indeed possible at times that the person concerned makes light of the interest of the given set-up even when nothing else is at stake. But there may also be times when there are other interests, say, the interest of truth or the interest of humanity in general, which may have a higher claim than the interest of the given set-up. And in that case it would be irrational, a piece of bigotry, on the part of anyone to keep on sticking to the interest of the given set-up. Further, as far as the above-mentioned second reason is concerned, quite simply a clear distinction should be made between the interest of a social set-up in which a person occupies a certain position and the interest of the authorities themselves in that set-up. While this person is, at least normally speaking, unquestionably justified in vindicating the interest of the set-up in which he occupies a certain position, he is under no obligation whatsoever towards vindicating the interest of the authorities themselves in that set-up. Therefore, one may say that the second reason is no reason at all against the public use of reason.

In this place I am tempted to make a psychological digression. I would like to mention some of the components which it is not unusual to find involved in the mental constitution of the authorities in a social set-up. Firstly, the authorities in a social set-up are inclined to take a person occupying a certain position in that set-up making a public use of reason as a personal affront. This fact has to do, although not always entirely, with the second reason which I have mentioned and discussed above against making a public use of reason. Secondly, these authorities are inclined to identify the interest of the given social set-up with their own interest, such that, if a person in that set-up does something which happens to affect them adversely, they take it as having been done against the set-up itself. Thirdly, they are inclined to believe that what proceeds from them, what they say or do, is rational by that fact alone and there is no need for any further discussion in the matter. Fourthly, when they do so, they are inclined to mention the following as some of the reasons in support of what they say or do: (i) they have to keep in mind the interest of the whole of the set-up, and what they are saying or doing is from that point of view; (ii) they have talked to various people in the set-up about the matter, and they find that what they are saying or doing is all right; and (iii) they have given deep thought to what they are saying or doing, and they see no reason why things should happen differently. Fifthly, the authorities concerned are inclined to treat a person in the set-up having a difference of opinion with them as an expression of his personal hostility towards them.

Let me continue with my psychological digression for a little more while. Let me now mention some of the components which again it is not unusual to find involved in the mental constitution of the members of a social set-up in relation to the authorities in that set-up. Firstly, there are members who are always inclined to go along with the authorities. If, for example, the authorities take a person occupying a certain position in the given set-up making a public use of reason as a personal affront to them, then these members do the same and when doing so they make their own contribution towards that second reason which I have mentioned above against making a public use of reason. Some of these members may try to give the impression of being on their own, but it does not take long to find out. Secondly, there are members who, with the zest of a new convert, are inclined to go along with the authorities, provided they benefit from them in one way or another, and who are equally vehemently inclined to be even foul towards them if that does not happen, more so if the benefits are withdrawn. Thirdly, there are members who are inclined to support or oppose the authorities depending upon their temperamental similarities or dissimilarities with them, respectively. Fourthly, there are members who, while on the whole being suspicious towards the authorities, are inclined to look at things on merit; they are inclined to support them when they think that they are doing the right thing; and they are inclined to oppose them when they think that they are doing the wrong thing. Fifthly, there are members who are inclined to have nothing to do with the authorities, or even with the social set-up of which they are members, except officially and that also in a minimal way. Sixthly, there are members who are inclined to be totally cynical towards the authorities and accordingly not to miss any opportunity in making them an object of their tirade. There are times when these members have in their mental constitution an element of seeming to be heroic in relation to the authorities.

Now, after this digression, let me go back to Kant's thesis about the public use of reason and my defence of this thesis. Imagine a social set-up, say, an academic set-up which I have mentioned before, in which a person who occupies a certain position in that set-up is debarred from making a public use of reason (or in which this person's making a public use of reason is at least seriously frowned upon). In other words, imagine this social set-up, in which, while being obliged to follow the requirements of his position in the interest of that set-up, the person concerned is not allowed to present for discussion before the people at large his view that what he is required to do may not be quite the right thing, may not be quite the truth, which (view) he may present as a member of human society in general and as a man of learning in the interest of truth. Then, imagine a social set-up, say, an academic set-up as before, in which a person occupying a certain position in that set-up, while being obliged to fulfil the requirements of his position, is allowed to do this. Needless to say, as I have maintained earlier, from the point of view of what is the right thing, from the point of truth, humanity in general would be richer in the latter case than in the former. Kant says: ". . . Shall not a society of clergymen, for example an ecclesiastical synod or a venerable presbytery (as the Dutch call it), be entitled to commit itself by oath to a certain unalterable set of doctrines, in order to secure for all time a constant guardianship over each of its members, and through them over the people? I reply that this is quite impossible. A contract of this kind, concluded with a view to preventing all further enlightenment of mankind for ever, is absolutely null and void, even if it is ratified by the supreme power, by Imperial Diets and the most solemn treaties. One age cannot enter into alliance on oath to put the next age in a position where it would be impossible for it to extend and correct its knowledge, particularly on such important matters, or to make any progress whatsoever in enlightenment. This would be a crime against human nature, whose original destiny lies precisely in such progress."[4]

Part Two

In Part One of this paper I have dealt with Kant's thesis about the public use of reason. In Part Two now I wish to deal with his thesis about the private use of reason, namely the thesis that a person occupying a certain position in a certain social set-up is obliged to obey the dictates of his position in that set-up. The question which I would like to ask is: is Kant justified in maintaining that this person is obliged to do so under all conditions?

Let me revert to S_1 and S_2 which I have mentioned before. S_1 is a certain academic set-up of which the person A is a member. S_2 is a certain social set-up the basic principles of which S_1 is obliged to follow and of which also A is a member. It is a dictate of S_1 that the members of a particular denomination be given preferential treatment in their admission to S_1; and by virtue of the fact that S_2 vindicates the position of S_1 it is a dictate of S_2 as well. I have defended Kant's thesis about the public use of reason through a discussion of this example. My question now is whether Kant is also justified in his thesis about the private use of reason in respect of that example, that is, whether he is also justified in maintaining that A is obliged to follow the dictate of giving preferential treatment to the members of a particular denomination in their admission to S_1 under all conditions.

It is evident that if Kant is not justified in his thesis about the private use of reason, as I think he is in his thesis about the public use of reason; that is to say, for example, if A justified in not following the dictate concerned under all conditions, then he would be justified in opposing this dictate, not merely in respect of saying, but also in respect of doing.

Now, in the preceding part of this paper, in making a public use of reason about the dictate concerned, A has argued the following: (a) it is most likely that giving preferential treatment to the members of the said denomination will put them in a state of mind where they think that they have already caught up with the rest, with the corollary that, among other things, S_1 and S_2 suffer in quality; and (b) again it is most likely that once this provision is there, they will want it to be perpetuated towards an easy fulfilment of their self-interest. Now, suppose that these apprehensions are no longer mere apprehensions, but they have come to be true. That is, the members of the said denomination have indeed been put into a state of mind where they think that they have already caught up with the rest with the corollary that, among other things, S_1 and S_2 are indeed suffering in quality, and, further, these members have indeed been doing their utmost for the perpetuation of the given provision towards an easy fulfilment of their self-interest. The question is: whether one would still, in the face of this condition obtaining, maintain that A follow the dictate concerned.

Let me mention one more example. It is once again a dictate of our academic set-up S_1 that in it a person is admitted on the basis of a certain formal interview. In an artificial setting this person is confronted with some people who put to him various questions to find out whatever they may be wanting to find out and this person is called upon to respond to these questions. Now, in making a public use of reason in connection with the present example, A contends as follows: (i) being in the situation in which they find themselves, neither the person who is being interviewed nor the people who are interviewing feel their normal or natural self. The former is overawed and the latter are basking in the assurance that nothing can go wrong for them, (ii) The two sides meet at an unequal footing, not in the sense that the former side knows less and the latter side knows more, but in the sense that while the former is constantly under suspense about whether it is right or wrong, the latter can all the time pretend that it knows, (iii) The people who interview have to have competence. That is to say, they have to know what they wish to find out as also how they can find that out. And besides, they have to have some of the moral qualities like impartiality, sympathy, and humility. But these qualities, whether of competence or the moral ones, are not easy to come by. Now, it is possible to engage A in a discussion. Thus the person B may accept all of A's contentions. But he may go on to argue that, in spite of these difficulties, one is able, and not quite infrequently, to make the right selection. A may not deny this. Now, suppose that A's apprehensions are no longer mere apprehensions, but they have come to be true; that is to say, while there may be occasions when there is a right selection, there are indeed occasions and occasions when there is not, in all likelihood for reasons of A's apprehensions. Would one still maintain that A obey the said dictate in an unqualified manner?

Now, this question as also the similar questions which I have raised about the first example are easily answered. The dictate of giving preferential treatment to the members of a certain denomination, who have long been disadvantaged, is there to enable them to catch up with the rest. But if it does not produce this result but the ones expressed by A's apprehensions, then it would evidently be irrational to obey this dictate. Likewise, the dictate of conducting a formal interview for admission to S_1 is admittedly there for being able to make the right selection. But if, while it may produce this result on some occasions, there are occasions and occasions when it does not produce this result, in all likelihood for reasons of A's apprehensions, then again it would evidently be irrational to obey this dictate.

I have mentioned two examples above to examine Kant's thesis about the private use of reason. I have argued in both the cases that there are occasions when one would be justified in not obeying the said dictates. And my argument in both the cases is one and the same, namely this: if there is a dictate on the basis that it will produce such and such result, and if it does not indeed produce that result, then one would evidently be justified in not obeying it.

Let me now mention the following two examples: (i) the dictate of a civil administration that any person who falls within its jurisdiction has to pay taxes; and (ii) the dictate of an army that any person who is its member has to obey the orders of his superiors. Both these examples are also included in Kant's long statement which I have quoted at the beginning of this paper. We already know from this statement that, while Kant would want public use of reason about these examples, he would not allow any deviation in respect of private use of reason about them.

The questions are: (i) is Kant justified in maintaining that a person who falls within the jurisdiction of a certain civil administration is obliged to obey its dictate of paying taxes under all conditions? and again (ii) is Kant justified in maintaining that a person who is a member of a certain army is obliged to follow its dictate of obeying the orders of his superiors under all conditions? Now, in considering these questions, both at the same time, I am not saying anything new, but treading on a ground all of which is by now quite familiar. It is indeed true, from the legal point of view, that the persons concerned have to obey their respective dictates. But, from the moral point of view, a case can be made out for their departing from them. The case is that if there is an unjust social order in conception or application, then one would be justified in non-cooperating with it. And two of the ways in which one may do so, wherever it is theoretically possible, are non-payment of taxes and non-compliance with the orders of the superiors in the army, although one may like to adopt these ways only in rather extreme circumstances.

In the preceding I have mentioned four examples to examine Kant's thesis about the private use of reason. As I have already said, in the case of the first two examples, I have argued that one is justified in not obeying a given dictate on utilitarian grounds, i.e., on grounds that it does not produce the result for which it is there. In the other two examples now, I have argued that one is justified in not obeying a given dictate on moral grounds, i.e., on grounds that given such-and-such situation one simply should not do such-and-such.

Imagine a social set-up: (i) in which a person who occupies a certain position in that set-up obeys its dictate which does not produce the expected result; or (ii) in which he willingly or unwillingly goes along with it even when it happens to be morally unjust and as an expression of this going along with it obeys its dictates. And then imagine a social set-up: (i) in which a person who occupies a certain position in that set-up does not obey its dictate which does not produce the expected result; or (ii) in which he does not go along with it when it happens to be morally unjust and as an expression of this not going along with it does not obey its dictate or dictates. Here it is evident, once again, that from the point of view of what is the right thing, from the point of truth, humanity in general will be richer in the latter case than in the former.

At the end of Part One of this paper, I have maintained that, from the point of view of what is the right thing, from the point of truth, humanity in general will be richer if a person who occupies a certain position in a certain social set-up is allowed to make a public use of reason. In the preceding paragraph now, I have maintained that, from that point of view, humanity in general will be richer if that person is allowed to make a deviation from a private use of reason under certain conditions. It is self-evident, then, that, from that same point of view, humanity in general will be so very much richer if both these possibilities are combined.

Part Three

In the beginning of Part One of this paper, I have said that, according to Kant, a person is enlightened, if he has acquired the resolution and courage to use his own understanding without the guidance of others.

I would like to ask: what exactly does Kant mean by the phrase "without the guidance of others," what exactly is his notion of "without the guidance of others," in this definition?

Kant does not formulate a definition of this phrase. But from what he says while talking of the reasons for a person remaining immature, remaining unable to use his own understanding without the guidance of others, we can extract an exact definition of the phrase. We can say that, according to him, it means, "without leaving, or not leaving, it to others to understand things for oneself." Kant mentions laziness and cowardice as the reasons for a person remaining immature. "Laziness and cowardice are the reasons why such a large proportion of men, even when nature has long emancipated them from alien guidance (*naturaliter majorennes*), nevertheless gladly remain immature for life. For the same reasons, it is all too easy for others to set themselves up as their guardians. It is so convenient to be immature! If I have a book to have understanding in place of me, a spiritual adviser to have conscience for me, a doctor to judge my diet for me, and so on, I need not make any efforts at all. I need not think, so long as I can pay; others will soon enough take the tiresome job over for me. The guardians who have kindly taken upon themselves the work of supervision will soon see to it that by far the largest part of mankind (including the entire fair sex) should consider the step forward to maturity not only as difficult but also as highly dangerous. Having first infatuated their domesticated animals, and carefully prevented the docile creatures from daring to take a single step without the leading strings to which they are tied, they next show them the danger which threatens them if they try to walk unaided."[5]

Thus we can say that, according to Kant, a person is enlightened, if he has acquired the resolution and courage to use his own understanding and not to leave it to others to understand things for him. And likewise we can go on to say here that, according to him, a person is immature, if he is unable to use his own understanding and leaves it to others to understand things for him.

Now, there is another sense in which the phrase "without the guidance of others" may be understood. In this sense the phrase means "without being helped in some way by others." A person does indeed go on to use his own understanding, but he has to be helped in some way in his going on to do so. There could be a theory, according to which a teacher has to help his pupils in some way towards enabling them to use their own understanding. Thus, for example, he may organize discussions for them for the purpose.

I come now to the next point which I wish to make in this part. I have already pointed out that, according to Kant, laziness and fear are the reasons for a person remaining immature. We have also seen that Kant mentions three examples in this connection, those of a book having understanding for me, spiritual adviser having conscience for me, and a doctor judging my diet for me. I would like to elucidate Kant's reasons a little more explicitly by means of two other examples, the first one in connection with the reasons of laziness and the second one in connection with the reason of fear. Both these examples have been taken from the academic world, where one would expect to find immaturity the least.

Suppose somebody is an idealist of one kind or another. To be specific: suppose somebody is a metaphysical idealist like Berkeley, i.e., a person who maintains that the world is nothing other than mental; or he is an epistemological idealist like Kant, i.e., a person who maintains that we do not know the world as it is in itself but as it is determined by us in some way or the other. Then it is possible that one is one thing or the other because Berkeley or Kant are like that. One does not himself take pains to argue out things for himself, but simply accepts them from them. There is another way in which laziness could manifest itself here. One does not study their writings for himself but picks up their positions from others who have not discussed them but just presented them in a simple and summary form. We find that this laziness is no less prevalent than the other.

Next, suppose that there is a thought in fashion. To be specific, suppose, under the impact of Wittgenstein's *Tractatus Logico-Philosophicus* on a certain interpretation, a humean empiricism or positivism is in fashion—namely the view that knowledge or significance are found only in the empirical or formal sciences. This may apply not merely to the general run of people but also to many of those from whom one would expect independent thinking. Then it is possible that one adheres to this position, not just because one is swayed to it, but out of explicit or implicit fear of being left out of fashion as well. One has not thought through the position on one's own. We find that Kant or Hegel or Marx make an impact, and then there are Kantians or Hegelians or Marxists galore. In this it is true that people are swept off their feet by the passing current. But it is no less true that they are explicitly or implicitly afraid to be cast aside. Even philosophy is not immune to falling a prey to the fashions of the day. An interesting aspect of all these people falling for a fashion is that they do not question their fundamentals with the same alacrity and thoroughness as they do those of others. They take their own fundamentals as so very unquestionable, and are inclined to ridicule all those who do not go along with them, to say the least.

In this third part, which may be treated as an appendix to this paper, I have so far articulated Kant's notion of "without the guidance of others" and elucidated a little more explicitly by means of some other illustrations than the ones which he mentions his thesis about laziness and fear being the causes of a person remaining immature. Now, there is one more point which I would like to make here. In the statement which I have reproduced from Kant in the third paragraph of this part, he maintains that for the same reasons of laziness and fear there are people who set themselves up as his guardians and keep him immature. I wish to say that there are other ways as well in which a person may be kept immature. Thus there are people in varied forms, especially including those who claim to be saviours, who go out of their way to condition him to a particular way of thinking and living and who look with intense disfavour at his thinking and living in his own way. We may call this way of keeping a person immature the doctrinaire way. Then there are people, including teachers in particular, who keep a person immature not for reasons of laziness and fear in him but in themselves. These guardians are not prepared to take the pains which thinking on one's own involves, and they are not prepared to take the risk of entering into uncharted territories of thought.

They are quite satisfied with simply transmitting bits of information already available.

Notes

1. *Kant's Political Writings* (edited with an introduction and notes by Hans Reiss, Cambridge University Press, 1970).
2. *Ibid.*, p. 55.
3. *Ibid.*, pp. 56–57.
4. *Ibid.*, p. 57.
5. *Ibid.*, p. 54.

10

Morality of Means

I WOULD LIKE to ask the question: how do we determine the morality of means? That is, how do we determine that the means which we have employed for realizing an end are of a moral nature? For the time being I define an end as an object which we desire to bring into existence. And I define the means as objects which are efficacious or productive of that end. I may now reformulate my question as follows: how do we determine that the means which we have employed for realizing an end are not only efficacious, but also moral?

It will be noted that the question which I have raised here is about how we determine the morality of means. It is not about how we determine the morality of ends.

Concerning the question which I have raised in the preceding, there is a view, according to which, the morality of means is dependent upon two factors. First, it is dependent upon the end in view being moral. Secondly, it is dependent upon the means which we have employed for realizing that end being efficacious. That is to say, it is dependent upon the efficacy of the means for a moral end. We can say that there is a view, according to which, the morality of means is nothing other than the efficacy of the means itself for a moral end. We can call this view the utilitarian or efficacy view of the morality of means.

Let me give some examples.

(i) Suppose that we desire to bring into existence a state of affairs in which a person, say A, does not take undue advantage of another person, say B, that is, a state of affairs in which there is no exploitation, which (state of affairs) we consider moral; and suppose that keeping A under constant threat of serious repercussions in case he takes undue advantage of B prevents him from taking undue advantage of B; then keeping A under constant threat of serious repercussions in case he takes undue advantage of B would be moral.

(ii) Suppose that we desire to bring into existence a state of affairs in which there is provision for the realization of the general welfare of the people, which (state of affairs) we consider moral; and suppose that some particular person (or body of persons) is found eminently capable of providing for the general welfare of the people, although at the same time he is well-known to indulge in corrupt practices; then keeping or having that person there would be moral.

(iii) Suppose that we desire to bring into existence a state of affairs in which there is no terrorizing of people by the terrorists to push their cause, whatever that cause may be, which (state of affairs) we consider moral; and suppose that terrorizing the terrorists themselves keeps them under check; then terrorizing the terrorists themselves would be moral.

(iv) Suppose that we desire to bring into existence a state of affairs in which we get rid of the authorities in a state which are plundering the state, so to say, which (state of affairs) we consider moral; and suppose that liquidating these authorities ultimately emerges as the only way of getting rid of them, as the only way of protecting the state from being plundered by them; then liquidating these authorities would be moral.

Let me take the third example mentioned in the preceding. According to this example, if preventing the terrorists from terrorizing the people is moral, and if terrorizing the terrorists themselves prevents them from terrorizing the people, then terrorizing the terrorists themselves is moral. Now, there is a tendency among many people, concerning the use of violence for getting things done, to believe that if this much of violence does not work, then more would do so; and if that much more violence does not work, then still more would do so; and so on. And these people persist with this belief in spite of constant failure, in spite of all the evidence to the contrary. I take it that, according to the utilitarian view of the morality of means, the use of violence (terrorizing the terrorists) would not be moral, whatever the strength of the belief, if this did not produce the desired result. We may go on to add that it would be totally foolhardy and the cause of any amount of unavoidable suffering.

Mill can be taken as a representative of the utilitarian view of the morality of means. We have his well-known thesis that happiness, by which he means pleasure and the absence of pain, is intrinsically desirable, in fact the only thing which is intrinsically desirable; and unhappiness, by which he means pain and the absence of pleasure, is intrinsically undesirable, in fact the only thing which is intrinsically undesirable. And, further, we have his well-known thesis that an action is right in proportion to which it produces happiness and wrong in proportion to which it produces unhappiness. That would mean that: (a) an action is right if it produces happiness; (b) it is more right if it produces more happiness; and (c) it is less right if it produces less happiness; and likewise: (a) an action is wrong if it produces unhappiness; (b) it is more wrong if it produces more unhappiness; and (c) it is less wrong if it produces less unhappiness. Or, in terms of Mill's definitions of happiness and unhappiness, his definitions of right action and wrong action would mean that: (a) an action is right if it produces pleasure and no pain; (b) it is more right if it produces more pleasure and less pain; and (c) it is less right if it produces less pleasure and more pain, but, still, less than the pleasure it produces; likewise: (a) an action is wrong if it produces pain and no pleasure; (b) it is more wrong if it produces more pain and less pleasure; and (c) it is less wrong if it produces less pain and more pleasure, but, still, less than the pain it produces; and an action is equally right and wrong if it produces the same amount of pleasure and pain.

I have mentioned above the utilitarian view of the morality of means as the efficacy of means for a moral end. In the preceding I have mentioned Mill's view that actions are right in proportion to which they produce happiness, and wrong in proportion to which they produce unhappiness. Now, I find that Mill's account of right and wrong actions can be applied to the utilitarian account of the morality (and, let me say, immorality) of means in the following way as well: we can say that, according to the utilitarian view, means are moral in proportion to which they produce a moral end, and immoral in proportion to which they produce an immoral end. That would mean that (a) means are moral if they produce a moral end; (b) they are more moral if they produce more of a moral end; and (c) they are less moral if they produce less of a moral end; and likewise: (a) means are immoral if they produce an immoral end; (b) they are more immoral if they produce more of an immoral end; and (c) they are less immoral if they produce less of an immoral end. Let me illustrate both these cases: (i) Suppose that preventing the terrorists from terrorizing the people is a moral end; and suppose that, in the first place, terrorizing the terrorists themselves prevents them from terrorizing the people for a shorter or longer period of time in word and deed; and, in the second place, persuading the terrorists, say, in the name of their causing suffering to innocent people, prevents them from terrorizing the people for a shorter or longer period of time in word, deed, and thought; then the second sort of means would be more moral as realizing more of the given moral end, and the first sort of means would be less moral as realizing less of the given moral end. And we can say that both the sorts of means would be moral as realizing the given moral end. (ii) Suppose that instigating the terrorists towards terrorizing the people is an immoral end; and suppose that, in the first place, giving financial support to the terrorists instigates them to terrorize the people while that support is there in word and deed; and, in the second place, brainwashing the terrorists instigates them towards terrorizing the people for a certain length of time in word, deed and thought; then the second sort of means would be more immoral as realizing more of the given immoral end, and the first sort of means would be less immoral as realizing less of the given immoral end. And we can say that both the sorts of means would be immoral as realizing the given immoral end.

Take the following cases: (i) suppose that preventing the terrorists from terrorizing the people is a moral end; and suppose that, in the first place, persuading the terrorists, say, in the name of their causing suffering to innocent people, prevents them from terrorizing the people in word, deed, and thought; and, in the second place, saying to them the right word at the right time produces exactly the same effect, but more efficiently, say, sooner. (ii) Suppose that instigating the terrorists towards terrorizing the people is an immoral end; and suppose that, in the first place, brainwashing the terrorists instigates them towards terrorizing the people in word, deed and thought; and, in the second place, saying to them the appropriate thing at the opportune moment produces exactly the same effect, but more efficiently, say, sooner. Then, it seems to me that, according to the utilitarian view of the morality of means, the second way in the former case would be more moral as being more efficacious in producing a moral end; and likewise the second way in the latter case would be more immoral as being more efficacious in producing an immoral end. And if I am indeed right in saying this, then we can reformulate the utilitarian view of the morality of means in the following manner: means are moral in proportion to which they produce a moral end, or in proportion to which they are efficacious in producing a moral end; and they are immoral in proportion to which they produce an immoral end, or in proportion to which they are efficacious in producing an immoral end.

Suppose that preventing the terrorists from terrorizing the people is a moral end which we wish to realize. Now, suppose that terrorizing the terrorists themselves, or persuading them, say, in the name of their causing suffering to innocent people, are the means through which we can realize that end. Then, rationally speaking, we would employ those means for realizing that end. But suppose that these are not the means through which we can realize that end. Then, rationally speaking, we would not employ those means for realizing that end. That means to say that the relevance of means, *qua* means, is entirely dependent upon the end which they realize, upon their being efficacious in realizing that end. We may call this the general theory of the relation of means and ends. Now, it is needless to say that, as undoubtedly subscribing to this theory of the relation of means and ends, the utilitarian view of the morality of means would be a part of the general theory of the relation of means and ends. But this view not only maintains this, but, as we have seen, it maintains, in addition, that means are moral by virtue of their being efficacious in realizing a moral end, and immoral by virtue of their being efficacious in realizing an immoral end. Thus the utilitarian view of the morality of means maintains two things: first, it maintains what it maintains as a part of the general theory of the relation of means and ends; and, secondly, it maintains what it maintains by itself.

Here we may define an end as a desired effect, and means as the cause which produces that effect. We may also express this by saying that means and ends are causes and effects, respectively, where effects are the desired effects.

Gandhi would not accept the utilitarian view of the morality of means. That is, he would not accept that means are there only as producing an end, as being efficacious in producing an end. And he would not accept that means are moral by virtue of their being efficacious in producing a moral end.

According to Gandhi, what means we adopt, on that will depend what end is achieved. Thus, for example, if we adopt violent means, which Gandhi would call bad or immoral, then one kind of end will be achieved. If we adopt non-violent means, which he would call good or moral, then another kind of end will be achieved. "As the means so the end."[1]

"Realization of the goal is in exact proportion to that of the means. This is a proposition which admits of no exception."[2] We cannot "get a rose through planting a noxious seed."[3] "The means may be likened to a seed, the end to a tree; and there is just the same inviolable connection between the means and the end as there is between the seed and the tree. I am not likely to obtain the result flowing from the worship of God by laying myself prostrate before Satan. If, therefore, anyone were to say I want to worship God; it does not matter that I do so by means of Satan,' it would be set down as ignorant folly. We reap exactly as we sow."[4] Gandhi mentions the example of an armed thief or robber and then mentions at some length what kind of result is achieved when we deal with him in a violent manner and what kind of result is achieved when we deal with him in a non-violent manner.

"That well-armed man has stolen your property; you have harboured the thought of his act; you are filled with anger; you argue that you want to punish that rogue, not for your own sake, but for the good of your neighbours; you have collected a number of armed men, you want to take his house by assault; he is duly informed of it, he runs away; he too is incensed. He collects his brother-neighbours, and sends you a defiant message that he will commit robbery in broad day-light. You are strong, you do not fear him, you are prepared to receive him. Meanwhile, the robber pesters your neighbours. They complain before you. You reply that you are doing all for their sake. You do not mind that your own goods have been stolen. Your neighbours reply that the robber never bothered them before, and that he commenced his depredations only after your declared hostilities against him. You are between Scylla and Charybdis. You are full of pity for the poor men. What they say is true. What are you to do? You will be disgraced if you now leave the robber alone. You, therefore, tell the poor men: 'Never mind. Come, my wealth is yours, I will give you arms, I will teach you how to use them; you should belabour the rogue; don't you leave him alone'. And so the battle grows; the robbers increase in numbers; your neighbours have deliberately put themselves to inconvenience. Thus the result of wanting to take revenge upon the robber is that you have disturbed your own peace; you are in perpetual fear of being robbed and assaulted; your courage has given way to cowardice.

"If you will patiently examine the argument, you will see that I have not overdrawn the picture. This is one of the means. Now, let us examine the other. You set this armed robber down as an ignorant brother; you intend to reason with him at a suitable opportunity; you argue that he is, after all, a fellow man; you do not know what prompted him to steal. You, therefore, decide that, when you can, you will destroy the man's motive for stealing. While you are reasoning with yourself, the man comes again to steal. Instead of being angry with him, you take pity on him. You think that this stealing habit must be a disease with him. Henceforth, you, therefore, keep your doors and windows open, you change your sleeping place, and you keep your things in a manner most accessible to him. The robber comes again and is confused as all this is new to him; nevertheless, he takes away your things. But his mind is agitated. He inquires about you in the village, he comes to learn about your broad and loving heart, he repents, he begs your pardon, returns you your things, and leaves off the stealing habit. He becomes your servant, and you find for him honourable employment. This is the second method. Thus, you see, different means have brought about totally different results."[5]

In brief, according to Gandhi:

(i) It is not the case that there is an end, and then we find out the means, any means whatsoever, entirely for their appropriateness in realizing that end.

(ii) It is not the case that the means are moral entirely as realizing a moral end.

(iii) What means we adopt will determine what end is achieved.

(iv) There are moral (say, non-violent) means, and there are immoral (say, violent) means. The former lead to the realization of a moral end, and the latter lead to the realization of an immoral end.

(v) That such and such means would lead to the realization of such and such end is a necessary proposition.

I would now like to make some comments upon Gandhi's above-mentioned view about the morality of means.

I have talked above of what I have called the general theory of the relation of means and ends. I have said that, according to this theory, the relevance of means, *qua* means, is entirely dependent upon the end which they produce, upon their being efficacious in producing an end. We can express this thesis by saying "as the end, so the means." Now, as we have seen before, according to Gandhi, it is not "as the end, so the means," but "as the means, so the end." In this connection I have mentioned his example of an armed thief, and what happens when we deal with him in a violent manner and what happens when we deal with him in a non-violent manner.

I find that this example which Gandhi mentions in support of his thesis "as the means, so the end" is an example of causal relation. That is, it is an example in which it is maintained that given such and such factors such and such result is produced. It is not an example of the relation of means and ends. We will have an example of the relation of means and ends when the following obtains: there is an effect which we desire to produce (an end); we find that such and such factors lead to the production of that effect (means); and, then, rationally speaking, we adopt those factors for producing that effect. Let me exemplify: (i) We desire that the armed thief would not steal any more by being converted; we find that the non-violent manner which Gandhi mentions leads to the production of that effect; and then, rationally speaking, we adopt that non-violent manner for producing that effect. (ii) We desire that the armed thief would not steal any more, whether by being converted or out of fear;

we find that the non-violent manner or violent manner which Gandhi mentions leads to the production of that effect; and then, rationally speaking, we adopt that non-violent manner or that violent manner for producing that effect.

We have seen that in cases of the relation of means and ends, the thesis which holds is "as the end, so the means." Gandhi's thesis of "as the means, so the end" does not hold there. But we find that Gandhi's thesis does indeed hold in cases of causal relation of general kind, cases like "terrorizing the terrorists prevents them from terrorizing the people," "treating a criminal non-violently leads to his conversion to the path of non-criminality," and "treating a criminal violently makes him a more hardened criminal." However, then, Gandhi's thesis would not be expressed in this way, but as "as the causes, so the effects."

Here I would like to make an observation. It seems to me that when Gandhi says "as the means, so the end," and not simply "as the causes, so the effects," there is a background of two presuppositions: first, the presupposition that there is such and such an end; and, secondly, the presupposition that there are such and such means which alone lead to the realization of that end. Let me elucidate these presuppositions by means of two examples, (a) There is the end of converting a criminal to give up his criminal ways, which we may call a moral end; and there are the non-violent means of dealing with a criminal, which one may call moral means and which, according to one, alone lead to the realization of that end. (b) There is the end of keeping a criminal constantly in a state of fear, which one may call an immoral, or at least not a moral, end; and there are the violent means of dealing with a criminal, which one may call immoral means and which, according to one, alone lead to the realization of that end. It is clear here that once there are these two presuppositions, there is Gandhi's thesis straightaway.

According to the utilitarian view of the morality of means, the morality of means is entirely dependent upon their producing a moral end. According to Gandhi, there are means which are moral in themselves. The question which I would like to ask here is: is Gandhi justified in saying that there are means which are moral in themselves? In case there are means which are moral in themselves, we can call these means as moral ends which are also means, or as means which are also moral ends.

Now, in answering the above-mentioned question, let me go back to Mill. And let me briefly state the following of the theses of his moral theory: (i) happiness, that is, pleasure and the absence of pain, is intrinsically desirable, in fact the only thing which is intrinsically desirable. I have already mentioned this thesis in section 1 above; (ii) All other things which are desirable, are desirable as means to producing happiness; (iii) Justice itself is desirable as means to producing happiness, as follows: it consists of an obligation to the performance of which somebody else has a right. And the reason why somebody has this right is its producing happiness, or general, happiness; (iv) The proposition that happiness is intrinsically desirable, in fact the only thing which is intrinsically desirable, is a self-evident proposition, to express oneself in that kind of way.

Now, there should be no difficulty in seeing the basis on which Mill maintains that happiness is intrinsically desirable, in fact the only thing which is intrinsically desirable; on that same basis one can maintain that justice, if nothing else, is also intrinsically desirable. That means to say that if one maintains, as Mill does, that the proposition that happiness is intrinsically desirable, in fact the only thing which is intrinsically desirable, is a self-evident proposition; then one can maintain with equal justification that the proposition that justice, if nothing else, is intrinsically desirable is also a self-evident proposition. I do not wish to deny here that justice may be a means to producing a moral end, say, the moral end of happiness, as Mill calls it. But if what I have said above is correct, then justice, if nothing else, may not only be a means to producing a moral end, it may be a moral end itself. And in that case Gandhi could be justified in saying that there are means which are moral in themselves, that is, means which are also moral ends. Gandhi takes non-violence to be one such means.

Let me make it clear here what I have, and what I have not, tried to prove in the preceding. I have not tried to show that Gandhi is justified in saying that there are means which are moral in themselves. All that I have tried to show is that, on a certain rather important theory, like that of Mill, Gandhi could be justified in saying that there are means which are moral in themselves.

There are terrorists who are terrorizing the people in order to push their cause. It is suggested that we can attain the moral end of preventing the terrorists from terrorizing the people by terrorizing the terrorists themselves. Now, suppose that these terrorists, or a number of them, make themselves immune to being terrorized; say, they train themselves to forming what are called suicide-squads. Then that means that the suggested means are rendered inefficacious (and thus irrelevant as means), and, as a result, as not producing the proposed end, they do not also acquire the quality of being moral.

Again, there are terrorists who are terrorizing the people to push their cause. It is suggested that we can attain the moral end of preventing the terrorists from terrorizing the people by persuading them, say, in the name of their causing suffering to innocent people. Now, suppose that these terrorists, or a number of them, make themselves immune to being persuaded by hardening themselves towards suffering. Then that means once more that the suggested means are rendered inefficacious (and thus irrelevant as means), although they may be moral in themselves.

Now, suppose that somebody makes use of the suggested means, whether of the former or the latter kind, although they have been rendered inefficacious (and thus irrelevant as means); then that person would be acting irrationally. I have already made this point in its positive form in section 1 of this paper. Consequently we can say that the first condition which needs to be fulfilled in determining the morality of means is that the means which we employ are efficacious (and thus relevant as means). This is the first thing we have to be sure of.

Suppose that we have at our disposal the following three kinds of means, all of which are equally efficacious in producing a moral end: (i) those which are moral; (ii) those which are immoral; and (iii) those which are neither moral nor immoral. Then it is evident that, from the moral point of view, we should employ the first kind of means, and should not employ the other two kinds of means, in producing that end. The first kind of means would have the quality of being moral by virtue of their producing a moral end; and, in addition, they would have the quality of being moral in themselves. Suppose that we have at our disposal the following two kinds of means which are equally efficacious in producing a moral end: (i) those which are immoral; and (ii) those which are neither moral nor immoral. Then it is evident that, from the moral point of view, we should employ the latter kind of means, and should not employ the former kind of means, in producing that end. The latter kind of means would have the quality of being moral by virtue of their producing a moral end, but they would not have the quality of being either moral or immoral in themselves. Suppose that we have at our disposal only the following kind of means, which is efficacious in producing a moral end—the means which are immoral. Then it is evident that, from the moral point of view, we should employ these means in producing that end, provided, of course, that the net immorality which may be there in our doing so is less than the immorality which may be there in our not doing anything in the matter. These means would have the quality of being moral by virtue of their producing a moral end, but they would have the quality of being immoral in themselves. We can say that, as far as the given three kinds of means are concerned, from the moral point of view, the world would be the best place if we employ the means which are moral, a better place if we employ the means which are neither moral nor immoral, and the worst place if we employ the means which are immoral, except, of course, when there is greater immorality as a result of our not doing anything in the matter.

There are terrorists who are terrorizing the people to push their cause. It is found that the method of terrorizing the terrorists themselves, which may by itself be an immoral method or one neither moral nor immoral, for attaining the moral end of preventing them from terrorizing the people is efficacious, but only over a relatively short period of time. In the beginning these terrorists withdraw, so to say, possibly out of fear of the harm which may be done to them or it may be for some other reason. But, in the course of time, they start reappearing. They may become less and less afraid. They may devise other ways of doing things; thus they may attack people without anyone being able to predict where and when and in what manner they would do so. Further, it is found that the method of persuading the terrorists, say, in the name of their causing suffering to innocent people, which may by itself be a moral method, for attaining the moral end of preventing them from terrorizing the people is also efficacious, but slow in progress, although it is effective over a longer period of time. In the beginning these terrorists may not take much notice of the suffering which they cause to innocent people. But as this suffering increases and more and more efforts are made to make them aware of it, they may relent and be prepared to explore other ways of pushing their cause, say, by talking things over. Then, given these two methods, from the moral point of view, one should do the following: employ the former method to whatever extent and for whatever period of time it is effective, but at the same time employ the latter method to supplement the other and hopefully to replace it as soon as possible; provided, of course, that the net immorality which may be there in employing the first method is less than the immorality which may be there in employing the second method alone from the beginning.

In the preceding I have mentioned two kinds of means for attaining the moral end of preventing the terrorists from terrorizing the people: those of terrorizing the terrorists themselves, and those of persuading them, say, in the name of their causing suffering to innocent people. I would like to mention here yet another kind of means, which may be used for attaining that end. These means consist of isolating the terrorists from the rest of the people, means which may be neither moral nor immoral in themselves. These means have the following ingredients: (i) the people will not provide the terrorists with physical support. That means to say that they will not make available to them a hiding place from their being found out; they will not give them money and material to build up; and they will not help them in respect of other ends which they may have; (ii) They will not provide them with moral support. That means to say that they will not only not encourage them in their activities, they will even look down upon what they have been doing; (iii) They will not hesitate to report regarding their whereabouts. Here there should be no difficulty in seeing that it is far, far from easy for people to do all that they have been required to do. Among other things, they run the real risk of losing their life and property. But they may be made somewhat willing by taking various steps. First, they should be ensured as much protection as possible against harassment by the terrorists. Secondly, they should be made aware that, in case they did not do all that they have been required to do, they would be treated as conspirators, and as such would be subject to due punishment. Thirdly, and most importantly, they should have the conviction that what they are doing is right. This conviction can be inculcated, in the first place, by presenting them with the true picture of the facts of the case, the exact cause which is dear to the terrorists and the points which are in favour of and those which are against that cause; and, in the second place, by truthfully telling them that all that could be done in considering that cause has been done, and the way is still open for further deliberation.

Needless to say that in case the third kind of means which I have mentioned above are efficacious, they will have the quality of being moral by virtue of their producing a moral end, but evidently they would not have the quality of being moral or immoral in themselves, on the assumption that they are neither moral nor immoral in themselves.

In the second section of this paper I have mentioned Gandhi's thesis that moral (say, non-violent) means produce a moral end, and immoral (say, violent) means produce an immoral end. In this connection, I have also mentioned his example of an armed thief, and his contention that if we treat this person in a non-violent way, then a non-violent end is produced; and if we treat him in a violent way, then a violent end is produced. I would like to examine here Gandhi's just-mentioned thesis. And, in doing so, I will take an example.

Suppose that the head of an institution is constantly bullying the people who work under him in order to have control over them. Now, anyone would easily find that the way in which this person is acting need not always produce the same kind of response among his subordinates, a violent response, as Gandhi would have it. It may produce a whole variety of responses among them. Here let me mention just three of those. Some subordinates may retaliate in kind; if the head of the institution bullies them, they reply by a violent agitation against him. Some subordinates may simply cow before that person. Some subordinates may see the harm which is being done to the institution by the way in which that person is acting and also by the ways in which the first two groups are responding; and he may try to persuade both the sides to adopt an attitude of willing cooperation on a footing of equality.

Likewise, suppose that the head of the institution is seeking the support of his subordinates in his work in order to carry them along with him. Now, again, anyone would easily find that this way in which this person is acting need not always produce the same kind of response among his subordinates, a non-violent response, as Gandhi would have it. It may produce a whole variety of responses. Here let me mention just two of those. Some subordinates may reciprocate. But some others may see it as a sign of weakness on the part of the head of the institution, and as a result they may adopt an attitude of domineering towards him.

In respect of the example of an armed thief which he mentions; Gandhi himself concedes the possibility of one affected party being led to adopt a non-violent attitude, and another affected party being led to adopt a violent attitude, towards that person's violent act of armed thievery.

I have said that a violent or non-violent act produces different kinds of responses. In saying this I do not wish to deny that it is rather common that a violent act produces a violent response, and a non-violent act produces a non-violent response. What I wish to deny is that they do so always, without exception, as Gandhi says.

It is found that the kind of response which the moral or immoral act produces in the people concerned may depend upon a number of factors. It may depend upon their temperament, their strategy, their cultural orientation, their natural constitution unless otherwise cultivated, or something else.

Here let me briefly state some of the main theses of this paper: (i) I have mentioned two of the views about how we determine the morality of means: the utilitarian view and the Gandhian view. According to the former, the morality of means is dependent upon their being efficacious in producing a moral end. According to the latter, this is not so. There are means which are moral in themselves. Further, it is not that the ends determine what means we are going to employ; it is the means which determine what ends are going to be produced. Thus moral means produce moral ends, and immoral means produce immoral ends. (ii) In order to determine the morality of means, the first thing which we have to be sure of is their efficacy in producing the proposed end. (iii) While there may be means which are moral in themselves, the morality of means is also, to some extent, dependent upon their efficacy in producing a moral end. (iv) Moral or immoral means may produce different kinds of ends, and not necessarily ends of some specific kinds. (v) One can work out an order of preference among the means to be employed in producing a moral end. It is also possible to say something about the application of means in accordance with their efficacy in producing a moral end.

Notes

1. *The Collected Works of Mahatma Gandhi* (New Delhi: The Publications Division, Ministry of Information and Broadcasting, Government of India), Vol. 24, p. 396.
2. *Ibid.*
3. Raghavan lyer, ed., *The Moral and Political Writings of Mahatma Gandhi* (Oxford: Clarendon Press, 1986), Vol. 1, p. 239.
4. *Ib'id.*, pp. 239–400.
5. *Ibid.*, pp. 241–42.

11

Knowledge and Morality

THERE ARE CERTAIN intellectual and moral qualities which a person who pursues knowledge (philosophical or scientific) generally needs to have. The intellectual qualities include the following: (i) a person who pursues knowledge should clarify his problem to himself and formulate it as exactly as possible; (ii) he should be as clear, precise, simple and straight as possible in his expression and use no jargon; (iii) he should find out, through his own reflection or discussion or in any other way, the various objections which may be raised against his position and give them due consideration; and (iv) he should accept his thesis, even after he has done his best to confirm it, only tentatively. However, it is not a part of my purpose in this paper to make a comprehensive or a somewhat comprehensive list of these intellectual qualities and deal with them at any length whatsoever. What I wish to do here is to mention several of the moral qualities and dwell upon them in some detail.

We find that there are various other problems as well concerning knowledge in connection with morality, like the problem of knowledge and its immoral use, or the problem of knowledge and employment of immoral means for its acquisition. In this paper I am not concerned with any of these other problems.

Now, I would mention and treat to some extent several of the moral qualities which a person who pursues knowledge needs, one by one.

(i) The first moral quality which I would like to mention and which a person who pursues knowledge needs is this. He should make sure that he is interested in the problem which he wants or undertakes to explore. It is clear here that if he is interested in that problem, then he will feel involved in it, and, as such, he will carry on his work enthusiastically. On the other hand, if he is not interested in it, then he will not feel involved in it, and as such either he will not carry on his work at all or do so only as a tedium.

One may have a problem in which one is interested or in which one comes to be interested; or one may have a problem in which one is not interested or in which one ceases to be interested. When one has a problem in which one is not interested or in which one ceases to be interested, then one may have it as a result of the sway of a fashion, or as a result of somebody else's influence or authority, or as a result of habituation, or as a result of something else like that. Let me illustrate all these theses:

(a) A proponent of the method of non-violence propounds that this method can be used even in the most violent situations. And then one asks oneself the question whether it can be used to combat terrorism, to combat people who have made up their minds for whatever reason to push their cause by striking terror. It does not matter in what degree. And if so, what form is it going to take? Is it, for example, going to take the form of somehow meeting these people and entering into a dialogue with them trying to dissuade them from what they have been doing, or even the form of self-sacrifice, if that becomes necessary?

(b) A proponent of the method of non-violence propounds that even self-sacrifice, if that becomes necessary, can be a form of this method. And then one asks oneself the question whether self-sacrifice, which undoubtedly involves violence done to oneself, can be a form of this method of non-violence.

(c) At a given point in time, it has become fashionable for people to engage themselves in a discussion of the relevance of the method of non-violence at that time. And then, as swayed by that fashion, one engages oneself in that same discussion. Or again at the same time or at some other time, under the influence of somebody whom one respects or as dictated by somebody who has authority over one, one once more engages oneself in that same discussion.

(d) It is possible that, in the course of time, as a result, say, of a continued failure in some rather difficult case as in the first example mentioned above, one either just gives up altogether or goes on tediously out of habituation or fear of public disrepute or something else of that sort. Or, it is possible that, in the course of time, while carrying on one's work as a result of the sway of a fashion or somebody else's influence or authority, one is struck by something, as, for example, in the third case mentioned above, one is struck by the possibility of our life being governed by the method of non-violence, and then one comes to be interested in that thing.

I have talked of one's interest-based problem or one's non--interest-based problem. When one is or comes to be interested in a problem as found in the first example mentioned above, I may call it a constructive interest-based problem. When one is or comes to be interested in a problem as found in the second example mentioned above, I may call it a critical interest-based problem. I may also call one's non-interest-based problem an interest-extraneous problem.

When one has an interest-based problem, then one has an internal urge to explore that problem without any ulterior considerations, like those of a desire to belong or fear or reward. That one has such an urge is discovered by means of an honest and repeated self-reflection over a period of time. It is discovered externally, although not unambiguously, by means of (i) the kinds of things which one says ("I am worried like hell about it," "I am quite excited about exploring it," "I cannot get over it," and so on); (ii) one's intense or continued absorption; and (iii) the kind of life which one is prepared to live, that is, one's being prepared to live a life of deprivation (witness Socrates). When one has a non-interest-based problem, then one does not have an internal urge to explore that problem without ulterior considerations, like those of a desire to belong or fear or reward. That one does not have such an urge is discovered once more by means of an honest and repeated self-reflection over a period of time, which may be longer here than before. Externally, however, there may be a good deal of overlapping between the marks in the present case and those in the earlier one

(ii) The second moral quality which I would like to mention and which a person who pursues knowledge needs is this: he should be determined to persevere in his work in face of things which threaten to bring it to a premature end. This moral quality itself makes plain what will happen if he does not have it, namely that he will not be able to go on and his work will come to a premature end.

The things which threaten to bring to a premature end the work of the person who pursues knowledge include: (a) rigours and strain of hard work, (b) difficulties, (c) disappointments or frustrations, and (d) dullness and vacuity. Let me explain these things one by one:

(a) Barring luck (or, they say, inspiration), there is no substitute for hard work in the pursuit of knowledge, as, I suppose, in any other human pursuit. And this hard work is no easy matter, but requires rigorous self-discipline. That is, it requires one's being able to resist many a temptation which will take one away from one's work, the temptation to stay longer in the warmth of one's bed in winter, the temptation to be with people whom one is fond of and so on; and it requires one's being able to tie oneself down to one's work whether or not one is in a mood to do so. And we find that this entire exercise does not leave the resources of one's body and mind unaffected.

(b) In the pursuit of knowledge there are difficulties and difficulties, sometimes of a rather serious nature, as, I suppose, in any other human pursuit. Here I would mention a few difficulties of a rather serious nature. In this paper itself I have talked of intellectual and moral qualities which are required for the pursuit of knowledge, and then, of course, I have talked of knowledge for the pursuit of which these qualities are required. Questions arise: what exactly is the distinction between these two kinds of qualities? And what exactly is meant by knowledge? In this paper I have avoided a discussion of these questions, simply assuming that one could do without that for the purposes of this paper. But somebody may insist upon some clarification. Further, there is the view that every member of a society, including a State, should be allowed to publicly discuss every matter, but at the same time he is under an obligation to fulfil the duties laid upon him by the society. Questions arise: should he be allowed to publicly discuss even those matters which in the interest of the society are strictly confidential? And should he be under an obligation to fulfil even those duties laid upon him by the society which he considers as violating, say, the principles of justice?

(c) In the pursuit of knowledge, there are not only difficulties even of a rather serious nature, there are also difficulties, which, according to all appearances, defy solution and consequently cause disappointment or frustration, as possibly in any other human pursuit. Here I would mention a couple of examples in this connection: (i) there is the view that, in knowledge, we can never be sure of getting at the object itself, because we can never be ultimately sure that our mind has not introduced some distortion in its relation to it. On the other hand, there is the view that, in knowledge, in the realms of science and common-sense, we always proceed on the assumption that we are dealing with the object itself, and just look at the results in these areas. The difficulty here whether, in knowledge, logic or science and common-sense are justified defies solution and consequently causes disappointment or frustration; (ii) there is an argument to the effect that a moral object, like any other object, is ultimately only known intuitively or through direct apprehension. But then there is the objection against this thesis that in that case there would be no objective criteria for settling disputes among conflicting intuitions. Again, the difficulty here about the inescapability of the intuitionistic thesis on the basis of a certain argument, but at the same time the non-availability of objective criteria for settling disputes among conflicting intuitions, defies solution as far as one can see and consequently causes disappointment or frustration.

Under 2(b) above, I have explained the difficulties including those of a rather serious nature which arise in the pursuit of knowledge. Under 2(c) above, I have explained the difficulties which arise in the pursuit of knowledge but which, according to all appearances, defy solution and consequently cause disappointment or frustration. One finds that the intensity of discomfort which we feel in the face of these difficulties would be reduced to some extent in the following way: (a) if we formulate as clearly and exactly as we can the difficulty with which we are faced, and then work out the direction or directions in which the solution to this difficulty may be looked for, and (b) if we believe that looking for a solution to this difficulty is a part of our common work.

(d) In the pursuit of knowledge, there are occasions when we experience dullness and even vacuity. This dullness consists in being rather bereft of ideas. This vacuity consists in being quite bereft of ideas. Both these things are brought about through an overuse of one's mind and lack of change mainly in one's routine of work. As we know, in the present situation, various things like rest, change of place, engagement in some other activity, confrontation with nature, and just idling away help.

(iii) The third moral quality which I would like to mention and which a person who pursues knowledge needs, is this: he should allow his work to take its own course and time; that is to say, he should be patient in his work. If he does not allow his work to take its own course and time, that is to say, if he is not patient in his work, for whatever reason, then his work is likely to suffer in a number of ways: he may make use of ideas which he has not yet fully clarified to himself; he may make use of expressions which do not fit in or which are not clear and exact; he may draw conclusions which do not follow; and so on.

Here I may elucidate the just-mentioned moral quality by means of an example. Under 2(c) above, in ultimately knowing a moral object, just as any other object, I have talked of the inescapability of the intuitionistic thesis on the basis of a certain argument, but at the same time the non-availability of objective criteria for settling disputes among conflicting intuitions. Now, in order to allow our work to take its own course in respect of getting at this situation, we will evidently have to do the following things: we will have to state the theses from which the intuitionistic thesis is said to follow, at the same time seeing that these theses are all right. We will have to see that the intuitionistic thesis which is said to follow from these theses does indeed follow from them. We will have to see that, given the intuitionistic thesis, there may be different intuitions, and, what is more, different conflicting intuitions. We will have to understand as clearly and exactly as possible the notion of objective criteria. We will have to see whether or not there are objective criteria in that sense for settling disputes among conflicting intuitions, given that there are conflicting intuitions following the intuitionistic thesis. And in case these objective criteria are not there, we may like to go on to explore whether there is something else which is not as good as these objective criteria, but which can save us to some extent from the chaos of conflicting intuitions. Further, as far as the question of allowing our work in respect of the abovementioned situation to take its own time is concerned, it is difficult to say in advance how much time it will take to do. For, firstly, we find that the different items of the said work are difficult in varying degrees, and it is difficult to say in advance how much time an item of work with that much of difficulty will take to do. And, secondly, we find that our mind may be in a different condition while doing different items of work, for example, having more clarity and concentration while doing one item of work and less while doing another, and it is difficult to say in advance how much time it will take to do such and such item of work in such and such condition of mind. All that we can do here is to make a general statement that we would need to devote less time if the difficulty is less and mind more fit, and more time if the difficulty is greater and mind less fit.

I take it as a part of the moral quality which I have mentioned in the present section that, even after this quality has been satisfied, that is, even after we have allowed our work to take its own course and time or have been patient in our work, we let it rest for a further period of time and we even distance ourselves from it in space for some time. That way we can hope to gain greater clarity, exactness, comprehension and connectedness, and even a better idea of its significance or lack of it.

(iv) The fourth moral quality which I would like to mention and which a person who pursues knowledge needs is this: he should do his best to understand a point of view which is different and opposite, and even to sympathise with it; that is to say, he should do his best to be tolerant towards such a point of view. If he does not do so, then he may miss out a point of view which may be correct or which may contribute to the emergence of a point of view which may be correct.

It is a failing on our part that when we are confronted with a point of view which is different and particularly which is opposite, we are irritated sooner or later and more or less; and there are occasions when even a bit of personal gulf threatens to make its appearance at least for a little while. It is also a failing on our part that when a different and particularly an opposite point of view is put forth in criticism of our own point of view, then there are occasions when we are inclined to take it as a restilt of some personal hostility, and sometimes we even tend to take it as a personal affront. In order to do away with these failings, we need to cultivate self-discipline, which is directed towards enabling us to determine the merit of a point of view in complete detachment from any personal element.

Let me take here the following situation: I have done as much thinking as I could possibly do about a certain point of view, and, as a result, I find it to be quite unassailable. For example, after utmost thought, I cannot help coming to the conclusion that what some society accepts as the right thing to do need not be the right thing to do, and, somewhat technically speaking, to say that it is is to commit the logical error of identifying an existing state of affairs with a desirable state of affairs. Likewise, after utmost thought, I cannot help coming to the conclusion that there are experiences, like the experience of being at ease or the experience of being ill at ease, and these experiences are not just some bodily behaviours, although, of course, some bodily behaviours may and do indeed accompany these experiences. Now, suppose that, in the face of this situation, somebody is still found to maintain a point of view which is different and opposite. Then, in keeping with the moral quality which I have mentioned in this section, would we still maintain that we should do our best to understand that point of view and even sympathise with it? I suggest that we may do so once or so more, in order to further confirm our point of view. But after that has been done, the only form, I think, which the said moral quality may now meaningfully take is that of keeping our mind open for some unforeseen eventuality which may call for a change.

(v) The fifth moral quality which I would like to mention and which a person who pursues knowledge needs is this: he should be ruthless, that is, totally unbiased, in his examination of people's positions, including his own. If he does not do so, then there is a real danger of extraneous elements intervening in his attainment of truth.

Take the following cases:

(a) We would rather that our own position was not subjected to a thorough examination and was accepted more or less as such. On account of our thinking well of our position, we even have the belief that it does not stand in need of being examined and can be accepted as such. As a matter of fact, we are annoyed and may also become aggressive when somebody finds fault with it. We are happy when it is praised, even in respect of something which we ourselves see as a weakness but which we then do not go on to point out.

(b) I can well imagine that we somehow come to fancy a certain position or a certain person who holds a certain position, and then towards the position which we come to fancy or the position which is held by the person whom we come to fancy, we adopt about the same attitudes which we do towards our own position and which I have mentioned under v (a) above. I can also well imagine that we somehow come to have an antipathy for a certain position or a certain person who holds a certain position, and then towards the position for which we come to have an antipathy or the position of a person for whom we come to have an antipathy, we adopt some such attitudes as the following: we would rather that it was rejected straightway; we consider it worthless and therefore as something which cannot be accepted; we are happy when somebody finds fault with it; we are unhappy when somebody praises it even for being on the way to establishing itself; and we are unhappy when somebody praises it even for some point of strength in it.

(c) We are afraid of, at least publicly, examining a position which happens to be fashionable. For we are afraid that, in examining this position, we are likely to be called a dunce, not being able to understand and appreciate what others are so clearly able to do; and we are even likely to be treated as an outcast.

(d) We are afraid of, again at least publicly, examining a position of a person who has made a name for himself, or whom we consider superior in wisdom, or who stands in some kind of relation of superiority to us, or who is likely to do us harm, or from whom we are likely to benefit; and there may be other people like that whose position we are afraid of examining.

I have mentioned some of the cases, but only some, which may stand in the way of our satisfying the moral quality which I have listed in this section, in the way of our being ruthless or totally unbiased in the examination of people's positions, including our own.

We find that in order to acquire the moral quality which I have mentioned in this section, we need to have several other moral qualities, like detachment (for which we need honesty), fearlessness, being prepared to be ridiculed, being prepared to go it alone, being prepared to suffer and being prepared for self-sacrifice.

(vi) The sixth moral quality which I would like to mention and which a person who pursues knowledge needs is this: he should have the awareness that he may have made some or the other mistake in the course of his work, that it is possible that his work is not worth much and that it is not worth much on the whole any way; that is to say, he should be humble about his work. In consequence of this awareness, he should be open-minded in respect of rectifying whatever mistake he may have made and doing the right thing. It is clear that if he does not have this moral quality, his work will continue to be beset with that mistake and he will not be able to attain knowledge.

Humility, which 1 have talked of in the above paragraph, does not mean that we have not worked harder than we have or have not acquired a stronger conviction than we have. To put the matter a little more elaborately than 1 have done in that same paragraph, it means that, despite the best efforts and the utmost conviction on our part: (a) we have the awareness that we may have gone wrong somewhere; for example, we may have taken something as an object of value which is not so, we may have taken something as justification for an object of value which is not all right, we may have considered something as a means to the realization of an object of value which is not the case, and we may have had only an inadequate comprehension of some notion which we may have made use of; (b) we have the awareness that what we have done may not be worth much, not only in the sense that it may have already been done by others and better, but also in the sense that it may not be worth much even otherwise; and (c) we have the awareness that what we have done is anyhow just a fraction of the stupendous work which is always waiting to be done.

Here let me take a slightly technical example of a belief, which is widespread, has a long history, has been much argued for and has been held with great firmness, but about which there is now an argument which leads us to say that it is erroneous. The belief is that a moral law ultimately derives from a psychological law or a social law or a religious law and so on; for example, we ought to work for our pleasure or preservation, because we just want our pleasure or preservation; we ought to be worthy of mutual trust, because the society of which we are members just looks at that sort of thing with approval; and we ought to treat all men as our brethren because our religion enjoins us to do that. The argument which is now there and which leads us to say that this belief is erroneous is simply and straightforwardly this, that what we ought to do does not follow or is not derivable from anything which just happens to be the case in this world, for instance, from what is just wanted or approved or enjoined, it does not matter by whom or what. The argument is not in the least aimed at showing that the various things of which it is said that we ought to do them are not among the things which we ought to do; it is entirely limited to maintaining that what we ought to do does not follow from what it is said to follow from.

In opposition to what is enjoined by the moral quality which I have mentioned in this section, a person who has the awareness that nothing can have gone wrong in the course of his work, and his work is worth much considered on the whole or otherwise and who, as a consequence, is close-minded about rectifying anything in his work, is, from the point of view of the pursuit of knowledge, dogmatic and self-conceited.

(vii) The seventh moral quality which I would like to mention and which a person who pursues knowledge needs is this: he should be prepared to suffer privations. If he does not have this moral quality, he would not be able to do his work or his ability to do his work would be more or less reduced.

Let me here mention some of the privations which a person who pursues knowledge should be prepared to suffer.

Did Aristotle say that a philosopher needs a hundred slaves to be able to do his work? However, it is immaterial for my present purpose to determine whether Aristotole really said so or not. The point is that, not just a philosopher, but any person who pursues knowledge should have the provision for the satisfaction of his basic needs to the extent that he can do his work more or less without worry. At the same time he should have at his disposal suitable, that is peaceful and healthy, conditions of work. In this connection one may add that his being close to nature would be further mentally refreshing, broadening and creative. This thought leads one to suggest incidentally that it would be a good idea if our places of learning were as close to mother nature as possible. Now, the various facilities which I have mentioned above and which a person who pursues knowledge should have may be made available to him socially or he may do something on his own to make them available to himself. But in case they do not become available to him whether in one way or the other even rather remotely in a measure in which he needs them, he should be prepared to do without them.

Further, there are various things in which a person who pursues knowledge need not be without interest; in fact in some of them he may have a good deal of interest. These things include the following: (a) having a social life, visiting people and having them visit him, attending social functions, being present in places where other people have gathered for change and amusement, having friends and spending time with them, and sharing in the life of one's kinspeople; (b) going here and going there, seeing new, different, strange, distant and attractive places, and seeing over and over again places which are familiar but which one is rather fond of; and (c) participating in one way or another in varied cultural life, going alone or along with other people to different places, imbibing the history of these places and the lives of the people who live there, and undertaking some or the other activity of an adventurous nature. Now, a person who pursues knowledge should be prepared to forgo these things, in which he may have some or a great deal of interest, at least to a certain extent.

(viii) The eighth and the last moral quality which I would like to mention and which a person who pursues knowledge needs is this: he should allow his work alone, and never considerations of any personal gain, to dictate to him the results of that work; that is to say, he should be entirely objective and unselfish in determining the results of his work. If he does not satisfy this moral quality, that is, if he does not allow his work alone to dictate to him the results of that work, but allows considerations of some or the other personal gain to intervene in the matter, then (a) he would not be able to devote undivided attention to his work, and (b) he would be prepared to make compromises in respect of the results of his work: he would be prepared to abandon the results of his work in case they happen to affect his personal interest adversely, and he would be prepared to arrive at results to which his work does not lead in case they happen to promote his personal interest. Needless to say, in that way truth will suffer.

There is no denying that a person who pursues knowledge generally has before his mind considerations of personal gain. He desires material benefits in the form of a greater financial yield or a higher professional position or something else of that kind. But more than this, he desires social recognition. He desires that his work receives as wide a publicity as possible, not merely for the reason that he finds a very wide forum for a discussion of his views, but also for the reason that he is known and admired here and he is known and admired there. He would not even mind if he is known and admired as an author of some important views, without people knowing what these views are. He desires that he is honoured as well. However, as I have mentioned before, a satisfaction of these desires should not be a determining factor in the results of his work. It may only be an incidental consequence of the work which he is doing.

12

Notes on Kant's Derivation of the Various Formulae of the Categorical Imperative

I

THE PRIMARY PURPOSE of this paper is a logical rather than an ethical one.[1] Strictly speaking, it is no more than to see how Kant obtains the various formulae of the Categorical Imperative in his *Groundwork of the Metaphysic of Morals*,[2] and to discuss the basis upon which he does so.[3]

I accept Paton's thesis that, in the *Groundwork*, Kant mentions five different formulae of the Categorical Imperative (although, explicitly or implicitly, he also speaks of them as being one or three or four).[4] For the purposes of the present paper, I will adopt Paton's statement of these formulae and also the titles which he gives to them. However, I will not adopt his system of their numeration; I will simply number them in serial order from one to five.[5]

II

The First Formula, the Formula of Universal Law, is stated as: act only on that maxim through which you can at the same time will that it should become a universal law.

Now, Kant may, without much difficulty, be said to deduce this formula, correctly, from: (1) his conception of (moral) duty as the necessitation to act on a maxim which can at the same time be willed as a universal law; and (2) his conception of an imperative as the formula of the necessitating command of duty. For all that this formula embodies is the expression in the form of an imperative, in the form of a categorical imperative, of the necessitating command of duty to act on a maxim which can at the same time be willed as a universal law (briefly speaking, of the universality of a maxim).[6]

III

The Second Formula, the Formula of the Law of Nature, is stated in the following manner: act as if the maxim of your action were to become through your will a universal law of nature.

Now, on page 52 = 421 of his *Groundwork*, Kant says in respect of this formula that in so far as the universality or the universal character of the causal law constitutes nature as regards its form (i.e. the form of nature), the Categorical Imperative (the universal imperative of duty), may also be stated as follows: act as if the maxim of your action were to become through your will a universal law of nature (or, in other words: act on the maxim which you can at the same time will to become a universal law of nature).

What exactly is Kant saying here? Apparently this: the universality of the causal law constitutes nature as regards its form; therefore, the Categorical Imperative (the universal imperative of duty) may also be stated as follows: act on the maxim which you can at the same time will to become a universal law of nature.

Now, I do not see how, on the basis of the first proposition in this argument, the restatement of the Categorical Imperative as given in the second proposition in it is possible. All that one may say, on the basis of the first proposition and what has hitherto been said about the Categorical Imperative in the First Formula, is that there is a similarity between the universality of the causal law which defines nature as regards its form, and the universality of the maxim of an action which defines morality. And therefore one may restate the Categorical Imperative, although I do not see what is really gained by doing so, as follows: act on the maxim which you can at the same time will to become a universal law, like a universal law of nature. Further, on page 71 = 431 of his *Groundwork*, with regard to the formula under consideration, Kant says that the Categorical Imperative (that is, the Second Formula of the Categorical Imperative) enjoins conformity of actions to universal law on the analogy of natural order.

Now, here Kant clearly conceives of the Formula of the Law of Nature as being analogical in character. But what is the analogy which he has in mind between what the Categorical Imperative enjoins and natural order? Kant does not elaborate his statement. But I cannot think of any other analogy than this: that the Categorical Imperative enjoins the pursuit of a universal law, just as natural order is governed by a universal law. And if this is so, then the Categorical Imperative may only be restated in the way in which I have done above, although, as I have also noted above, it seems to me to be a redundant exercise.

Still further, on page 81 = 437 of the *Groundwork*, in connection with the same formula, Kant says that, because the maxim of an action which a will can will as a universal law is analogous to a universal law which constitutes the formal aspect of nature, the Categorical Imperative may also be expressed as follows: act on that maxim which can at the same time have for its object itself as a universal law of nature (or, in other words: act on the maxim which you can at the same time will to become a universal law of nature).

Now, here again Kant clearly conceives of the Formula of the Law of Nature as analogical in character. And it is also clear,

I think, that the analogy which he has in mind is that of the universality of a law in both cases. And if that is so, then the Categorical Imperative may only be restated, although at the cost of redundancy, as I have restated it above.

In brief, one may say that all that Kant would seem to be doing in the Second Formula of the Categorical Imperative is to compare the Categorical Imperative with a law of nature in terms of their universality, and therefore to be doing something which is entirely redundant. And hence this Second Formula of the Categorical Imperative would seem to deserve to be completely left out.[7]

IV

The Third Formula, the Formula of the End in Itself, is: act in such a way that you treat humanity, whether in your own person or in the person of any other, never simply as a means, but always at the same time as an end.

Now, in order to discover the argument through which Kant may be said to obtain this formula, I would begin with an analysis of the four paragraphs on pages 63–7 = 427–9 of his *Groundwork*, in which Kant deals with this formula. The first of these paragraphs starts with the sentence, 'The will is conceived as a power of determining oneself to action in accordance with the idea of certain laws.' And the fourth ends with the sentence, 'We will now consider whether this can be carried out in practice.'

In the first paragraph, Kant may be said to be saying the following things: (i) to have a will is to be capable of determining oneself to action in accordance with the idea of certain laws; (ii) a rational being alone has a will; (iii) an end is what a will adopts as the ground of its determination: (iv) an end is equally valid for all rational beings, if it is given by reason alone; (v) there may be subjective ends, which are set by impulse; these are relative ends, because they depend upon the special characteristics of the person who has them, or, there may be objective ends, which are set by the motive valid for every rational being; and (vi) practical principles which abstract from all subjective ends are formal; those which do not do so but depend upon them are material. The latter are not universal, but of the nature of hypothetical imperatives.

In the second paragraph, Kant may be said to be saying the following: suppose there is something which has absolute value, which is an end in itself; then that alone would be able to function as the ground of a categorical imperative.

It will be noted here that the point which Kant makes in this paragraph may be said to have been made already in the preceding paragraph. In the preceding paragraph, it may be said to have been maintained already that the end set by reason, which is an absolute end, is the basis of a universal practical law or categorical imperative.

The third paragraph contains the following main theses: (i) a rational being, which includes man, is an end in himself, not merely a means; that is, he is to be viewed at the same time as an end; (ii) the objects of inclinations have only a conditional or relative value; they have value only as objects of these inclinations; so also the inclinations themselves. Kant calls the objects of inclinations, which have only relative value, things. On the other hand, rational beings, who by virtue of their being rational are ends in themselves, are called persons; they are objects of reverence; and (iii) one could say that rational beings, who are called persons, are not merely subjective ends but objective ends as well.

I think that here it will be conceded without any difficulty that when in this paragraph Kant calls a rational being (which includes man) an end in himself, he is not using the term 'end' in the sense defined in the first paragraph, in the sense of what a will adopts as the ground of its determination. As distinguished from this, he now simply calls anything which possesses rationality, that is, basically rationality itself, an end in itself.

I take the following to be the quintessence of the fourth paragraph: thus if there is to be a supreme practical principle or categorical imperative, we must obtain it from the idea of something as an end in itself. This imperative is: 'act in such a way that you always treat humanity, whether in your own person or in the person of any other, never simply as a means, but always at the same time as an end'.

Now, Kant has already maintained in the first paragraph that we obtain, or must obtain, the Categorical Imperative on the basis of the concept of an end in itself. Thus no new point has been made in the first sentence of the above passage.

The question of treating a rational being, and therefore a human being, as an end in himself arises because Kant may be said to have maintained already in the third paragraph that rationality is an end in itself: rationality is an end in itself; therefore, anything which possesses rationality, an action, an entity or being, is an end in itself. As a result, one may say that the Third Formula of the Categorical Imperative has been stated in a derivative form, with reference to something, an entity or being, which embodies rationality, and not with reference to rationality itself. Stated in its original form, it should read in some such form as follows: act in such a way that you treat rationality never simply as a means, but always at the same time as an end.

Now, on the basis of the above analysis of the four paragraphs under consideration, my construction of the argument from which Kant may be said to obtain the Third Formula is as follows:

Premise 1: one may have an end set by one's impulse, i.e. a subjective or relative end. Or, one may have an end set by one's reason, i.e. an objective or absolute end. While the former end would be the basis of a hypothetical imperative, the latter end would be the basis of a categorical imperative;

Premise 2: a rational being, whether perfect or imperfect, which includes man, is never simply a means, but always at the same time an end, by virtue of the fact that he is rational;

Conclusion 1: therefore, the Categorical Imperative: that we treat a rational being, whether perfect or imperfect, which includes man, never simply as a means, but always at the same time as an end;

Conclusion 2: hence, the Third Formula of the Categorical Imperative: act in such a way that you always treat humanity, whether in your own person or in the person of any other, never simply as a means, but always at the same time as an end.

Now, as regards the first premise in this argument, I would like to ask the following questions: (1) What exactly is meant by an end set by reason? (2) Is an end set by reason of the nature of an objective end? And how? (3) Does the concept of an objective end function as the basis of a categorical imperative? Now, as to the first of these questions: an end set by reason would mean an end set by that faculty which consists in being able to act on a maxim which can at the same time be willed as a universal law. (This end, I suppose, would always be an action.) As to the second question: if a maxim which can at the same time be willed as a universal law is objectively valid, i.e. it is a principle of action which not only I adopt, but other rational beings ought to adopt as well; that is, briefly speaking, if reason is the source of objective validity, then an end set by reason would be objectively valid, would be an objective end. And as to the third question: if one may say, generally speaking, that a categorical imperative expresses what is objectively valid, then one may say that a categorical imperative expresses an objective end.

Thus one may say that the first premise, at least as far as it would seem to be relevant for our present purpose, is all right on the basis of a certain assumption or assumptions.

As regards the second premise: if reason is the source of objective validity, then a rational being, *qua* rational, may obviously be said to have objective validity. But it is not at all clear here in what sense Kant calls a rational being an objective *end*, although it is clear that he cannot call him an objective *end* in the sense in which the term end has been used in the first premise, i.e. in the sense of what a will adopts as the ground of its determination. However, in so far as Kant calls a rational being an objective end by virtue of the fact that he is rational, he may be said to call rationality itself an objective end. But if he simply calls a rational being, or rather rationality itself, an objective *end*, that would make the second premise a purely arbitrary verbal thesis. And in that case we would obtain the Third Formula from the First Formula straightaway with the aid of this arbitrary verbal thesis.

As regards the conclusions of the argument under consideration: if one is justified in saying that in the second premise Kant calls rationality itself an objective end, then the Third Formula is stated in a derivative and not in the original form, with reference to something (a being) which has rationality and not with reference to rationality itself. Stated in the original form, it would read as follows: act in such a way that you treat rationality never simply as a means, but always at the same time as an end. On the whole, one may say that given the second premise as it is, the first premise is quite unnecessary. And then the Third Formula needs to be stated in an altered form, in a more fundamental way. Explicitly stated, the argument leading to the Third Formula would be:

> act on a maxim which can at the same time be willed as a universal law (i.e. act rationally);
>
> (First Formula)
>
> rationality is to be viewed, never simply as a means, but always at the same time as an end;
>
> (An arbitrary verbal thesis)

therefore, act in such a way that you treat rationality never simply as a means, but always at the same time as an end.

On page 80 = 436 of his *Groundwork*, Kant says that a rational being, by virtue of being rational, is an objective end, and must be so treated.

Now, the first part of this statement is essentially the same as the second premise mentioned above. And the Third Formula mentioned therein, which has been stated here in a derivative form, follows from the First Formula together with the second premise, as has been shown in the argument just explicated.

On pages 82–3 = 437–8, I take Kant to be saying basically the following things: (i) a rational being is distinguished from all other beings by the fact that he sets himself an end, which Kant calls the matter of a rational being (of a good will); and (ii) a rational being, *qua* rational, sets himself an objective end. Now, according to Kant, a rational being alone, by virtue of the fact that he is rational, can be an objective end.

Now, the first statement in this passage can be left out of consideration here, because it does not form part of any argument from which Kant may be said to derive the Third Formula. The second statement is included in the first premise mentioned above. Thus, again, we obtain the Third Formula by combining the First Formula with the second premise.

V

The Fourth Formula, the Formula of Autonomy, is: act in such a way that your will can regard itself at the same time as making universal law through its maxims.

Now, on pages 70–1 = 431–2 of his *Groundwork*, in connection with this formula, Kant may be said to say the following: according to the First Formula, the Formula of Universal Law, the ground of a moral law lies in universality; according to the

Third Formula, the Formula of the End in Itself, the ground of a moral law lies in treating a rational being as an end in himself, as an objective end. From here (hieraus) there follows the Fourth Formula, the Formula of Autonomy, namely 'the Idea of the will of every rational being as a will which makes universal law', or, according to which, the ground of a moral law lies in the will of every rational being being a will which makes universal law, or simply, lies in being made by a rational will.

Stated somewhat briefly, the argument contained here is:

> the ground of a moral law lies in universality;
>
> (First Formula)
>
> the ground of a moral law lies in treating a rational being as an end in himself, as an objective end;
>
> (Third Formula)
>
> therefore, the ground of a moral law lies in being made by a rational will.
>
> (Fourth Formula)

Now, there should be no difficulty in seeing here that the Fourth Formula does not follow from the First Formula and the Third Formula as contended above. That is, from the idea of a moral law being universal and the idea of a moral law as involving treating a rational being as an end in himself or as an objective end, the idea of a moral law as being made by a rational will obviously does not follow.

Further, on pages 71–3 = 431–3 of his *Groundwork*, in connection with the Fourth Formula which we have just been discussing, Kant says that this formula follows from the concept of the Categorical Imperative itself, because (i) it cannot be based on any extrinsic interest, as in that case we would have only a hypothetical imperative, and (ii) it must involve internal determination or self-determination of a rational will, as in that case alone we would have a categorical imperative.

Now, Kant is justified in saying that a categorical imperative cannot be based on any extrinsic interest, because in that case we would have only a hypothetical imperative. But it is no more than an assumption with Kant that an imperative would be categorical if it involved internal determination or self-determination of a rational will, if it was made by a rational will. And it is an assumption, because, according to Kant, if we exclude extrinsic interest, inclination, as the source of a categorical principle of action, then the one and only source from which it could emanate would be internal determination, determination of will by means of reason.

In short, while the negative part of Kant's argument to show that the Fourth Formula follows from the concept of the Categorical Imperative is justified, its positive part is no more than a piece of assumption.

Still further, on page 76 = 434 of his *Groundwork*, in respect of the Fourth Formula, Kant says that it follows from the First Formula as follows:

> an action is moral if the maxim of that action is such that it can at the same time be a universal law (or rather that it can at the same time be willed as a universal law);
>
> (First Formula)
>
> therefore, an action is moral if the maxim of that action is such that the will (or rational will) can regard itself as at the same time making a universal law through or by means of it.
>
> (Fourth Formula)

Now, does the Fourth Formula follow from the First Formula as contended in this argument?

One may say that the Fourth Formula follows from the First Formula if, in the First Formula, in the phrase 'can at the same time be willed as a universal', we replace the term 'willed' by its meaning in Kant as 'conceived as one's own', or 'considered as of one's own conception'. For, then, from the First Formula, 'An action is moral if the maxim of that action can at the same time be willed as a universal law', we obtain 'An action is moral if the maxim of that action is such that it can at the same time be considered as a universal law of will's/one's own conception', which is what the Fourth Formula is.

But we find that on the basis of the course suggested above, what we have here, strictly speaking, is a case not of inference, but of the restatement of one statement by means of another, of the First Formula by means of the Fourth Formula, through the substitution of a term by what is said to constitute its meaning.

And still further, on page 83 = 438 of his *Groundwork*, in respect of the Fourth Formula, Kant says that the Fourth Formula follows from the Third Formula in the following way:

> a rational being is distinguished as an end in himself by virtue of the fact that he makes universal law through his maxims;
>
> a rational being is an end in himself;
>
> therefore, he makes universal law through his maxims (to which, of course, as a rational being, he is subject).

Now, here the Fourth Formula does not follow from the Third Formula by itself, but in combination with an additional premise, the first premise. The first premise itself, as far as I can see, is introduced here for the first time, apparently as a purely arbitrary verbal thesis. But, of course, once this arbitrary verbal thesis is given, the Fourth Formula follows from the Third Formula in combination with it.

On the whole, one may say that Kant tries to infer the Fourth Formula: (i) from a combination of the First Formula and the Third Formula; (ii) from the concept of the Categorical Imperative itself; (iii) from the First Formula alone; and (iv) from the Third Formula alone.

The first attempt does not succeed. The second attempt succeeds by means of an assumption. The third attempt turns out, on the basis of a suggestion through which alone it had some chance of success, not, strictly speaking, to be an inference. That means that Kant does not really succeed in inferring the Fourth Formula in any of the ways mentioned above.[8]

VI

The Fifth Formula, the Formula of the Kingdom of Ends, is: act in such a way that you are always through your maxims a law-making member in a universal kingdom of ends.

Now, on page 74 = 433 of his *Groundwork*, in connection with this formula, Kant says the following: the concept of a rational being as making universal law leads to the concept of a kingdom of ends. A 'kingdom' is defined as (a) a systematic union (b) of different rational beings (c) under common laws. That is, we would have a kingdom if (i) there were different rational beings, and (ii) they were governed by common laws. Now, since rational beings are objective or universally valid ends by virtue of their being determined by reason, or, let us say, by universally or commonly applicable laws, a whole of these rational beings as objective ends would constitute a kingdom or kingdom of ends. In brief, one may say that the concept of rational beings as objective ends as constituting a kingdom or kingdom of ends follows from: (i) the concept of kingdom as described above; and (ii) the concept of rational being as objective end as one who is determined by universally or commonly applicable laws.

Now, here Kant begins with the claim that there is some close connection between the concept of a rational being as making universal law by his maxims and the concept of a kingdom of ends. But he actually goes on to derive the concept of rational beings as objective ends as constituting a kingdom of ends from his concept of kingdom and his concept of rational beings as objective ends as being determined by universally or commonly applicable laws. And there is no doubt that from the latter two concepts the former concept does follow. Now, take the Fifth Formula: act as if you were through your maxims always a law-making member of a universal kingdom of ends. It is clearly not obtained on the basis of the above derivation, i.e. it clearly does not follow from Kant's concept of kingdom and the Third Formula.

Further, on page 83 = 438 of his *Groundwork*, in respect of the Formula of the Kingdom of Ends, Kant says the following:

> rational beings make their (own) (universal) laws;
>
> therefore, a world of rational beings constitutes a kingdom of ends;
>
> hence, the Formula of the Kingdom of Ends: act as if (in such a way that) you were through your maxims always a law-making member in a universal kingdom of ends.

Now, here an attempt is made to derive the Formula of the Kingdom of Ends from the Formula of Autonomy. But it is clear that the former formula does not follow from the latter formula by itself. Two other premises, both of which are found in Kant and have been made use of earlier, are required. The complete argument would be as follows:

> a 'kingdom' is defined as a union of rational beings under common laws;
>
> (An arbitrary verbal definition)
>
> by virtue of his making universal law, a rational being is an end in himself;
>
> (An arbitrary verbal thesis)
>
> rational beings make their (own) (universal) laws; therefore, rational beings constitute a kingdom of ends;
>
> hence, the Formula of the Kingdom of Ends: act in such a way that you are always through your maxims a law-making member of a kingdom of ends.

In short, one may say that Kant does not succeed in deriving the Formula of the Kingdom of Ends from the Formula of Autonomy by itself. He can succeed in doing so only with the aid of an arbitrary verbal definition and an arbitrary verbal thesis.

On the whole, one may say that Kant tries to deduce the Formula of the Kingdom of Ends: (i) from his definition of 'kingdom' and the Formula of the End in Itself; and (ii) from the Formula of Autonomy. In the former attempt he obviously fails; in the latter attempt he can succeed only with the aid of an arbitrary verbal definition and an arbitrary verbal thesis.

VII

To summarize my conclusions concerning Kant's derivation of the various formulae of the Categorical Imperative:

1. Given Kant's concept of duty and his concept of imperative, the First Formula follows.
2. The Second Formula, which simply says that the moral law resembles a law of nature by virtue of both of them being universal, is entirely redundant and deserves to be completely left out.
3. The Third Formula follows from the First Formula in combination with an arbitrary verbal thesis, and is stated in a derivative form.
4. An attempt is made to derive the Fourth Formula: (i) from a combination of the First Formula and the Third Formula; (ii) from the concept of the Categorical Imperative itself; (iii) from the First Formula alone; and (iv) from the Third Formula alone. The first attempt does not succeed. The second attempt succeeds with the help of an assumption. The third attempt involves a restatement of, rather than an inference from, the First Formula. The fourth attempt succeeds with the aid of an arbitrary verbal thesis.
5. An attempt is made to derive the Fifth Formula: (a) from the Third Formula and a certain concept of kingdom; and (b) from the Fourth Formula. The first attempt does not succeed. The second attempt succeeds with the aid of an arbitrary verbal definition and an arbitrary verbal thesis.

In short, one may say that leaving aside the First Formula, and the Second Formula as being entirely redundant, the other formulae either do not follow or they follow with the aid of additional premises.

VIII

In the first section of this paper I said, in agreement with Paton, that in his *Groundwork*, Kant mentions five different formulae of the Categorical Imperative (although, explicitly or implicitly, he also speaks of them as being one or three or four).

The preceding deliberations enable us to decide exactly how many distinct formulae there are here really or ultimately.

> The First Formula conveys the idea of the *universality* of the maxim of an action. (1)

> The Second Formula does not convey any new idea; it simply compares the moral law with a law of nature in that both of them are universal. Thus the Second Formula can be subsumed under the First.

> The Third Formula conveys the idea of *treating humanity never simply as a means, but always at the same time as an end*, which is a distinct idea. (2)

The Fourth Formula conveys the idea of the *making of universal law through one's maxims*. But as, in Kant, the idea of being able to will the maxim of one's action as a universal law can be understood as the idea of being able to consider the maxim of one's action as a universal law of one's own conception, through the substitution of the term 'will' by its meaning, the Fourth Formula and the First Formula may be said to be conveying the same idea, namely the idea of being able to will the maxim of one's action as a universal law, or the idea of being able to consider the maxim of one's action as a universal law of one's own conception/the idea of being able to regard oneself as the maker of a universal law through one's maxim.

The Fifth Formula conveys the idea of *making universal law through one's maxim in a kingdom of ends*. The first part of this idea is clearly the same as the idea conveyed by the Fourth Formula. Now, Kant defines 'kingdom' in a particular manner, as the union of rational beings under common laws; and he simply calls rational beings as the makers of universal laws through their maxims ends or ends in themselves. As a result, the second part of the idea conveyed by the Fifth Formula does not convey a new idea; it is merely a new way of describing the idea conveyed by the first part of the Fourth Formula, a new way of describing rational beings as the makers of the universal, commonly applicable, laws through their maxims.

Consequently, the five formulae which Kant mentions are really or ultimately neither five nor one nor three nor four; they are two. That is, they basically convey two ideas only: (1) the idea, differently expressed, of the universality of the maxim of one's action, or of the universal law through the maxim of one's action, or of making universal law through the maxim of one's action in a kingdom of ends; and (2) the idea of treating humanity never simply as a means, but always at the same time as an end.

Notes

1. I am extremely grateful to J. T. Wilcox and W. H. Mueller for the several comments which they have made on this paper. I have taken them into consideration and reviewed my paper in the light of them. If I have stuck to my position at several places, I hope that more than obstinacy is responsible for it.
2. Translated by H. J. Paton, Hutchinson's University Library (London: Hutchinson, 1948).
3. On page 80 = 436 of his *Groundwork*, Kant maintains that a certain formula of the Categorical Imperative contains its form, a certain formula its matter, and a certain formula its complete determination. On page 79 = 436, he maintains that each of the formulae contains its complete determination. On pages 80–1 = 436–7, he maintains that certain of the formulae bring a certain formula nearer to intuition (although all of them are so many ways of saying the same thing). It

is not a part of my present purpose to deal with any of these three theses in any way. Further, I have said that, in this paper, I will be confining myself to dealing with Kant's derivation of the various formulae of the Categorical Imperative as found in his *Groundwork*, and in that work only. I will not be dealing with his other ethical writings, including the *Critique of Practical Reason*, in that connection.

4. A clear distinction should be made between the following: (1) the number of formulae of the Categorical Imperative which Kant actually mentions, and the number of formulae which, explicitly or implicitly, he says that he mentions; and (2) the number of formulae to which Kant-interpreters find the number of formulae which he actually mentions ultimately reducible. There may sometimes be a tendency among the interpreters to confuse these two things. That Kant mentions five different formulae can be easily seen, on the one hand, from the fact that he does mention them (see pages 52 = 421; 66–7 = 429; 70 = 431; 76 = 434; and 83 = 438); and, on the other hand, from the fact that he argues in connection with the derivation of all of them, as will be sufficiently borne out in the course of the present paper. For Kant's saying, explicitly or implicitly, that there are one or three or four formulae, see pages 52 = 421 and pages 79–81 = 436–7. Regarding the number of formulae to which, according to Kant-interpreters, the number of formulae which Kant actually mentions are ultimately reducible, there are different views. Thus, for example, according to Paton, they are in a way ultimately reducible to three (H. J. Paton, *The Categorical Imperative: A Study in Kant's Moral Philosophy*, Hutchinson's University Library (London: Hutchinson, 1946). More recently: according to Rollin, they are ultimately reducible to one ("There is only one Categorical Imperative', *Kant-Studien*, 73 (1982), pp. 291–320); according to Philip Stratton-Lake, they are ultimately reducible to three ('Formulating Categorical Imperatives', *Kant-Studien*, 83 (1993), pp. 317–40); and according to Paul Guyer, they are ultimately reducible to four ("The Possibility of the Categorical Imperative', *Philosophical Review*, 104(3) pp. 353–84). In the course of the present paper, as a result of a step-by-step discussion of all the various things which Kant says in connection with the derivation of the various formulae which he actually mentions, I have myself come to the conclusion that they are ultimately reducible to two.

5. Paton, *The Categorical Imperative*, op cit., p. 129.

6. *Groundwork*, pp. 51–2 = 420–1.

7. In his article 'Formulating Categorical Imperatives', Stratton-Lake does not consider the Formula of the Law of Nature to be distinct from the Formula of Universal Law. For, as he says, in the *Critique of Practical Reason*, Kant calls the Formula of the Law of Nature as being just the typic of the Formula of Universal Law ('Formulating Categorical Imperatives,' pp. 322–3). I have tried to show here that one would be justified in not considering the Formula of the Law of Nature as distinct from the Formula of Universal Law even on the basis of what Kant says in the *Groundwork* in this connection. Stratton-Lake does not take into consideration what Kant says there on the matter.
8. In 'Formulating Categorical Imperatives', Stratton-Lake does not consider the Formula of Autonomy as distinct from the Formula of Universal Law. What he says there amounts to saying that the Formula of Universal Law entails the Formula of Autonomy (p. 325). Now, I do not see how this is the case. In his *The Concept of the Categorical Imperative*, T. C. Williams makes the same point (Oxford: Clarendon Press, 1968, p. 30). I have tried to show here that Kant attempts to deduce the Formula of Autonomy in a number of ways, including the one which Stratton-Lake mentions, but unsuccessfully. And I have tried to show that the only method by which Kant can succeed is the replacement of the term 'will' in the Formula of Universal Law by its meaning in Kant as 'conceive as one's own'. But then we will not have an inference but a restatement.

13

Telling a Lie

I

TELLING A LIE may be defined as a person's stating the facts to be other than what they actually are, knowing that he is stating the facts to be other than what they actually are; or, as a person's stating something to be the case, knowing that what he is stating to be the case is other than what is actually the case.

A person may tell a lie in so many words, or not in so many words. Thus, for example, the persons A and B are involved in doing something conjointly. However, the people somehow believe that A alone is involved in doing it, and therefore they blame him alone for something that may have gone wrong with it. B does not say anything in the matter. Now, it seems to me that B's not saying anything in the matter is as good as his saying that he is not involved in doing it, knowing that he is involved in doing it, and thus it is as good as his telling a lie. It will be seen that in not saying anything in the matter and consequently telling a lie, B is also disowning collective responsibility and as a result betraying A's trust.

Telling a lie may be distinguished from the following: (1) saying what is false; (2) making a mistake; (3) misrepresenting something or somebody; (4) deceiving somebody else (in one sense); (5) being crooked; (6) concealing, or avoiding telling, the truth; (7) exaggerating; (8) being just so much story-telling; (9) telling a half-truth; (10) avoiding giving an answer; (11) rumouring; (12) saying something which is not warranted by the facts of the case; (13) giving an answer which is no answer; and (14) boasting.

(1) Saying what is false is a person's saying what is not the case. This is not done knowingly, but, say, on the basis of misperception, or fallacious reasoning, or hearsay, or unpreparedness or unwillingness to find out.

(2) Making a mistake is a person's doing something which he should not have done, or his not doing something which he should have done, as a result of a failure of proper understanding on his part.

(3) Misrepresenting something or somebody is a person's saying something about something or somebody which is not the case, or which he knows not to be the case; or misrepresenting something or somebody is a person's saying something about something or somebody which is false, or which is a lie.

(4) Deceiving somebody else (in one sense) is (a) a person's making somebody else believe what is not the case, or (b) a person's making somebody else not believe what is the case.

A person may deceive somebody else in a variety of ways, say, by talking ambiguously, or through telling a lie, or through telling a lie repeatedly, or by means of propaganda, or by concealing the truth.

Let me mention here an example of a person's deceiving somebody else by talking ambiguously. In the *Mahabharata*, Drona asks Yudhishthira, whom he trusted because of his righteousness, whether his (Drona's) son, Aswatthama, had really been killed in the battle. Yudhishthira tells Drona that Aswatthama had been killed; and then he goes on to add in a voice hardly audible that the elephant Aswatthama had been killed. It has been said that this was the only lie which Yudhishthira ever spoke. However, I find that here Yudhishthira did not tell a lie. He spoke the truth; Aswatthama, although the elephant Aswatthama, had indeed been killed. What he did was to deceive Drona into believing that his son had been killed, by talking ambiguously about Aswatthama. It is true that Yudhishthira tried to remove this ambiguity by saying that the elephant Aswatthama had been killed, but in a voice which was hardly audible. This was plainly a case of being crooked. One would have already noticed that, in not speaking in clear terms, Yudhishthira also betrayed Drona's trust in him. Thus, what we have in the course of Yudhishthira's short speech is (a) his trying to deceive Drona by talking ambiguously; and; in addition, (b) his being crooked, and (c) his betrayal of Drona's trust in him.

(5) Being crooked is a person's being dishonest.

I have already mentioned an example of being crooked under the above-mentioned head 'Deceiving somebody else (in one sense).' I have said that Yudhishthira was being crooked in telling Drona that it was the elephant Aswatthama which had been killed, but telling him this in a voice which was hardly audible.

(6) Concealing, or avoiding telling, the truth is as good as a person's telling a lie, although not in so many words; that is, it is as good as a person's (knowingly)saying that nothing is the matter when something is the matter, although not in so many words.

(7) Exaggerating is a person's more or less wittingly or unwittingly, overlooking the facts of the case, and presenting something as being in some sense more than it actually is. To the extent one overlooks the facts of the case, and presents something as being in some sense more than it actually is, wittingly, exaggerating is a case of telling a lie.

(8) Being just so much story-telling is a person's knowingly or unknowingly talking imaginarily or fictitiously or about things which may have no relation with reality.

(9) Telling a half-truth is a person's telling a part of the truth, but not telling some other part of the truth which is of vital importance.

Somebody who does not know the whole truth, would evidently have a highly mistaken notion of the whole truth, if he is told only a half-truth.

One may tell a half-truth deliberately or undeliberately. When one tells a half-truth deliberately, then one is telling a lie about that part of the truth which is of vital importance, although not in so many words. Telling a half-truth deliberately is the same thing as concealing, or avoiding telling, that part of the truth which is of vital importance. (See '(6)' above, 'Concealing, or avoiding telling, the truth.')

(10) Avoiding giving an answer is this: in response to a question, a person's neither speaking the truth nor telling a lie, but, say, keeping quiet or attempting diversions aimed at showing that he was not interested in answering that question.

(11) Rumouring is a person's spreading report without checking the truth of that report.

It is astonishing how many people find rumouring titillating, and also how many of them find it titillating to be the recipients of rumouring. In fact, the area of rumouring would be a rather rich area of investigation.

(12) Saying something which is not warranted by the facts of the case is, to say it in only slightly different words, a person's saying something which the facts of the case do not support.

Saying something which is not warranted by the facts of the case, that is, saying something which the facts of the case do not support, is saying something which is not the case, and this means that it is saying something which is false.

One says something which is not warranted by the facts of the case, that is, one says something which is false, say, on the basis of misperception, or fallacious reasoning, or hearsay, or unpreparedness or unwillingness to find out. (See '(1)' above, 'What is false.')

Saying something which is not warranted by the facts of the case, knowing that one is saying something which is not warranted by the facts of the case, is a case of telling a lie. (See the definition of telling a lie above.)

(13) Giving an answer which is no answer is this: in response to a question, a person's saying something which is no answer to that question, but is of the nature of sidetracking.

In giving an answer which is no answer, one does not deny that something is the case. One simply refuses to take cognisance of something being or not being the case.

(14) Boasting is a person's speaking in praise of himself for one thing or another, say, for something which he has done, or even for something which he has not done but which he would like it to be known that he has done it; or for something which he has, or even for something which he does not have but which he would like it to be known that he has it; or for his knowing such and such people, or even for his not knowing such and such people but he would like it to be known that he knows such and such people (for example, name-dropping).

One may boast in so many words or not in so many words. Boasting is a case of telling a lie, whatever else it may be, when one boasts for something being the case which is not the case, knowing that he is boasting for something being the case which is not the case.

II

Generally speaking, the notion of telling a lie is said to belong to the moral realm. Here two things are said about it. Firstly, there is the view that there is the moral law that one should not tell a lie. Kant is a well-known representative of this view. Secondly, there is the view that there are exceptions to the moral law that one should not tell a lie, just as there are exceptions to many other moral laws. This view is commonly held. I will mention examples in respect of both these views. In doing so I will be moving within a familiar territory.

I will begin with mentioning some examples in respect of the first view, that is, examples where, following the first view, in telling a lie one would be doing something which one ought not to do from the moral point of view, or which it is immoral to do.

(1) The first example which I am going to mention here is an extended and slightly modified version of the example which I have mentioned at the beginning of this paper. The persons A

and B are involved in doing something conjointly, say, in producing a report on the state of the institution of which they are members. The report contains a certain amount of criticism of those in authority, and as a result it arouses hostility of these people. In order that he is not affected adversely, B tells a lie. He says that, although he was a member of the team which was to produce that report, he was not actually involved in producing it; A alone was responsible for doing so.

(2) In a certain society, those of its classes of people which have somehow suffered great deprivation over a long period of time are provided with special benefits in order to ameliorate their lot. Thus there is a reservation of seats for them in educational institutions, and they receive a considerable amount of material help while they are there. There is a reservation of seats for them in matters of appointment. There is free or highly subsidized medical aid for them in public hospitals. Now, various people who do not belong to the classes just-mentioned but who would like to take advantage of the special benefits given to these classes tell a lie. They adopt all kinds of dubious ways towards showing that they also belong to these classes.

(3) Somebody has had, say, a cataract operation. However, there are certain complications. Thus there is swelling in the eye which has been operated upon and this swelling refuses to subside; there is the dislocation of the lens which has been put in the eye; and, more seriously, the vision in the eye is becoming weaker with passage of time. But the doctor, in order to protect himself against something that may have gone wrong with the operation, tells a lie. He says to the patient that everything is all right; and that he (the patient) is simply being misled into believing all sorts of things and is a victim of his own psychology.

(4) Some article is selling well in the market. It has been produced by a well-known firm. Now, a trader, in order to make much and easy money, tells a lie. He produces an article apparently similar to the one which is selling well and which has been produced by that well-known firm, and tells the customers that the article which he has himself produced has been produced by

that well-known firm. He may do so by putting the mark of that well-known firm on his own article.

I will now mention some examples in respect of the abovementioned second view (the view that there are exceptions to the moral law that one should not tell a lie); that is, examples where, following the second view, in telling a lie one would not be doing something which one ought not do or which it is immoral to do. There are two kinds of cases here. Firstly, there are cases in which in telling a lie one would be doing something which is of a moral nature. And, secondly, there are cases in which in telling a lie one would be doing something which is not of an immoral nature. The first three examples which I am going to mention relate to the first kind of cases; and the other three examples which I am going to mention relate to the second kind of cases.

(i) The persons A and B are very close to one another. A is B's dear teacher, and B is A's dear pupil. After several years, A, who is now old and weak, along with his wife is going to visit for some reason the place where B lives. He would very much like B to meet him and his wife on their arrival in that place. B has every intention of doing so, and is in fact keenly looking forward to doing so. But when the time comes, he quite inexplicably completely forgets the whole thing. Now, he could go to A, explain everything and apologise. However, A is an exceptionally sensitive person, and B knows that he would be shocked to hear that B was not there because he had forgotten to do so. As a result, B finds himself left with no alternative except to tell a lie. He says to A, when he meets him, that he is sorry that he could not make it, because he had to be away from the place on some pressing business and at a very short notice.

(ii) The person C is looking after his children, who have lost their mother. He is himself suffering from some painful and possibly incurable ailment. But he would not like his children, who have already lost their mother when they were still relatively young, to have an inkling of it. On occasions when the children see signs of their father not feeling quite well, they ask him how he is, and he tells them a lie. He says to them that he is all right. He would like, while he is there, that his children are happy as far as possible, and he is able to provide for their future as much as possible.

(iii) The person D has gone far, far away from home on some rather important work. However, in his absence, there is a tragedy in the family. He makes his usual enquiry from home, from wherever he is, whether everything was all right. Now, in order not to disturb him in the important work in which he is engaged so far away from home, the people in the family tell him a lie. They say to him that everything was all right, except, of course, those minor irritants which are taking place in a family all the time, but which are not worth bothering about.

(iv) The person E is an insistent, and not always a welcome, visitor. He would come and stay on, even if the family have some other plans of their own or have visitors with whom they would like to be by themselves. On some occasion, when they are settling down to doing something by themselves, they see this visitor making his way to them. And then they find that they simply have to tell him a lie. They tell him that they have to be going somewhere, and as a result they are rather busy preparing for it.

(v) The person F goes to attend a party. Going by his past experience, he expects this party to be in no way very different from the other of these parties. There would be a good deal of talking; the children would be playing among themselves, of course, making a certain amount of noise; there would be feasting; and so on. But when F arrives there, he is met with deafening noise. There is a band playing, and it is left to them to make as much noise as they like; in fact, the louder, the more welcome. And the people are themselves shouting, trying their best to keep pace with the band. F finds the whole scene unexpectedly unpleasant and nerve-shattering. And so he decides to tell a lie. He tells the host that he is sorry that he has to leave early, because he has to attend a couple of other parties as well.

(vi) The person G is an ambitious person, and as a result, irrespective of his level of competence, he would like to do one thing or another to acquire public recognition. He approaches the person H, whom he considers as his friend but who himself sees no such relationship between them, in whatever place the latter may be living, and suggests to him the various things which he would like him to do in that place to bring him (G) into prominence there. H does not respond to G's request. And when they happen to meet, he tells him a lie. He tells him that he is sorry that he cannot do anything in the matter because he is caught up in his own rather serious problems.

III

In the preceding section of this paper, I have been concerned with the thesis of the moral role or function of the notion of telling a lie in our life. According to this thesis, the moral role is the major role which the notion of telling a lie plays in our life; by and large, to talk of the notion of telling a lie is to have before one's mind its moral role. However, we find that the moral role is not the only major, let alone the only, role, which the notion of telling a lie plays in our life; it plays many other roles as well. I am going to mention only some of them. (1) A role, which may not be very far behind the moral role, which the notion of telling a lie plays in our life is its role in our life of politeness. (2) There are occasions when telling a lie is a folly; and there are occasions when not telling a lie is a folly. (3) There are occasions when telling a lie is just a matter of joke. (4) There are occasions when telling a lie is an expression of our concern and affection for somebody. We find that these other roles, at least collectively, which the notion of telling a lie plays in our life, may be as prominent as the moral role. We also find that, in virtue of some of these other roles, the notion of telling a lie has additional respectability, that is, in addition to the respectability which it has in virtue of there being times when telling a lie is not of an immoral nature. Telling a lie is not always an object of condemnation; often enough it is also an object of appreciation. In the following part of this section, I would mention examples in respect of the above-mentioned four roles which the notion of telling a lie plays in our life; and I would mention these examples in respect of these four roles in the order in which these roles are given above.

(1) It will be noted that a good deal of our life of politeness takes place through our telling a lie. It will also be noted that telling a lie in the life of politeness is not really telling a lie; it is a polite way of doing something or saying something else. (The role of telling a lie in our life of politeness could be a theme of enquiry by itself.) Let me now mention a few examples.

(i) The person I is invited to attend some function. But I is not inclined to go. And so he informs the people concerned that, although he would very much like to come, he is not able to do so on account of some preoccupation. Here telling a lie is a polite way of saying that one does not want to come or is not interested in coming. The people who have some experience of I in the matter would also interpret it in that way.

(ii) The person J has something, which the person K would like to borrow from him. But J would not like to lend it to K (or to anybody else for that matter). And so he tells K that he is sorry that he cannot lend it to him, because he is needing it himself all the time. Here telling a lie is a polite way of saying that one does not want to lend something which he has.

(iii) The person L would like to give something as a present to the person M. But M is not at all keen to have it for whatever reason. But he knows that L would be hurt if he did not accept it, and he would be happy if he accepted it. And so M accepts L's present and says to him that he is so very happy to have it. Here telling a lie is a polite way of going along for one reason or another.

(iv) The person N writes to the publishers of a book to allow him to publish a translation of that book. After some hesitation, the publishers give him the permission. However, in the course of time, in a state of sheer negligence or what can only be called a state of madness, he destroys the permission. And then he writes to the publishers once more for the permission. He says to them that he has misplaced the permission which they had kindly given him and is not able to trace it anywhere, and, therefore, he would be grateful to them if they give him another permission. Here telling a lie is a polite way of saying that something has gone wrong.

(v) The person O visits a place after a long time; and, while he is there, he makes it a point to meet several of his friends. Later on, the friend P comes to know of O having been there, and he is annoyed that O did not meet him, and complains to him about it. And then O tells P a lie. He says to him that he is sorry that he did not meet him, but, knowing that P was a rather busy person, he did not want to disturb him. Here telling a lie is a polite way of saying or confessing that things had gone wrong.

(2) I am going to mention two examples here; the first example is about telling a lie being a folly; and the second example is about not telling a lie being a folly.

(i) A person has developed some extremely serious, and possibly some terminal, malady. The members of the family, out of concern for him, tell him a lie about it. They tell him, even invoking the name of a doctor, that there is nothing very serious with him, and he should be all right soon. However, there is, or is emerging, a view, according to which, telling this person a lie is a folly. According to this view, this person should know exactly what the matter with him is, so that he knows exactly what all he is required or expected to do to get well or face the worst.

(ii) The person Q borrows things from just anybody, but never returns them. This is well-known. On some occasion, he asks the person R to lend something to him. Now, knowing things, R considers it a folly to lend it to him; unless, of course, he is prepared to forgo what he lends, and this he is not prepared to do. And as a result, he considers it a folly not to tell a lie, if by doing so one can escape lending the thing to him. And so he tells

R a lie. He says to him, say, that he does not have the thing which he has asked him to lend.

(3) I will mention here two examples of telling a lie as a matter of joke.

(i) The person S is infatuated with the person T, without the latter having the slightest inkling of the former's condition, or even without her having the least awareness of his existence. Some friends of S decide to have some fun at his expense. They write a letter to him, as if it has been written by T herself. In this letter they represent T as saying to S something to the following effect: 'I am deeply in love with you. Now and again I have tried to give you an indication in that direction, but you have not taken any notice. Kindly do something in the matter, so that my anxiety can be set at rest.' It is not for us to worry here about what happens to S after he receives this letter. I only wish to say at present that in the given case telling a lie is just a matter of joke.

(ii) The person U is fond of children and is easily able to establish a rapport with them. He is playing with the child V. He tells her, in fun, that there is a cat behind her. V, in a state of something of a panic, looks behind her, finds that there is nothing, and is a little embarrassed. U tells V that he was only trying to make an 'April fool' of her. U repeats the game at some other time, but this time V is already wiser.

(4) I will mention here just one example of telling a lie as an expression of one's concern and affection for somebody.

The persons W and X are lovers. Each of them would like to do something for the other. They sit down to a meal. Both of them are excessively fond of some item in the meal. But W says to X that she is not feeling like eating that item; she would be happy if X could take it, otherwise it would be wasted. X says to W that he was himself going to say exactly the same thing to her. It is not for us to worry here about how they work out things. What I wish to say is that their telling a lie is an expression of their concern and affection for one another.

While talking of telling a lie in our life of politeness, I have said that there telling a lie is not really telling a lie, but a polite way of doing something or saying something else. We now find that, in telling a lie as a matter of joke, once again, telling a lie is not really telling a lie; it is a way of having fun. And, likewise, in telling a lie as an expression of one's concern and affection for somebody, telling a lie is not really telling a lie; it is a way of caring for somebody or saying that one cares for somebody.

IV

In this section, I wish to deal with a problem which is not directly connected with the notion of telling a lie. But I find that the notion of telling a lie enables us to discuss this problem rather well. This problem relates to moral knowledge. It is about how we know a moral law, like 'Do not tell a lie' or 'Do not tell a lie except under conditions x.' I find that, in our moral deliberations, the problem of moral knowledge is no less important than the problem of the foundation of morality. However, somehow for sometime these problems have received very little attention in philosophy.

Take the following two cases:

(i) The chief of a state is charged with monumental corruption. There is more than a *prima facie* case against him in this connection. Now, in his anxiety to clear his name and believing that the people would be taken in, he declares to them, on oath, that he is completely innocent and is not at all involved in any corrupt practices. He goes on to say, showing how hurt he is, that it is his enemies who are responsible for dragging him into the whole affair. However, in the course of time, the charges against him are found to be conclusively established.

(ii) There is communal violence in some area. Members of community C1 are after members of community C2, for the simple reason that they are members of C2. It does not matter to them whether members of C2 whom they are after have harmed members of C1 or are innocent. It is enough that they are members of C2. The person Y, who is a member of C2 and is innocent, has found shelter with his friend Z, who is a member of C1. Members of C1, with some suspicion in their mind, come to Z and ask him whether Y was staying with him. Z answers in the negative. We need not worry at the moment about what follows.

Now, being confronted with the above-mentioned first case, that is, with the case of the chief of a state, who has been charged with monumental corruption and who is also later on found to be guilty of that charge, telling a lie that he is not involved in corrupt practices; we find that we are simply morally shocked at that. We say how, for heaven's sake, he could tell that blatant lie. (We find that we are also morally shocked at that chief of a state being involved in that corruption. But for the time being I am only taking the case of our being morally shocked at his telling that lie.) Likewise, being confronted with the above-mentioned second case, that is, with the case of Z's telling a lie in order to protect the life of innocent Y; we find that we simply morally approve of Z's telling that lie. We say that Z has acted in a morally right manner in telling that lie. We find that we are morally shocked at the first case, and we morally approve of the second case; and I do not know how to deny this.

At least on the face of it, there is a similarity between these cases, and, say, the cases in which we are confronted with certain objects and then characterize them as red, or hot, or loud. The similarity is this: in all these cases we are confronted with such and such objects, and then apparently as a result of this confrontation, and not as a result of something else, we characterize them in such and such ways (as morally shocking, or morally approvable, or red, or hot, or loud). Thus we do not characterize them in such and such ways because we want to characterize them in those ways. There is no urge on our part to tell a story. Here it does not matter that in one case there are physical objects, and in the other case there are what may be called moral objects. Here it does not also matter that in relation to physical objects there are sense-organs, but in relation to moral objects there are no what may be called moral organs.

A word of explanation here. I have said that we are confronted with such and such objects, and then we characterize them in such and such ways. It may be asked in this place: what does 'we' in this statement stand for? It does not stand for a group of people, large or small. It does not also stand for a number of people, large or small. It stands for any number of people, from one to all. The important thing is that whatever 'we' in the given statement stands for, whether for one or more than one person, that by itself has no significance whatsoever for the truth of our characterization.

Now, I have said that we are confronted with such and such objects, and then apparently as a result of this confrontation, and not as a result of something else, we characterize them in such and such ways. The question arises: how do we know that when we characterize these objects in these ways, we are doing so purely and simply as a result of this confrontation, and not as a result of something else, not even partly in that way? That something else because of which we characterize these objects in these ways may not be that we want to characterize them in these ways, that we want to tell a story. It may be something other than this. How do we know that it is nothing else whatsoever?

Now, I have not tried to find out what all can be imagined to fall under that something else, on account of which, and not purely and simply out of confrontation, we may characterize such and such objects in such and such ways. But there is one thing which we can well imagine, which in fact we even know well, to fall under that something else. This thing is of the subjective kind. Thus we can say that when we characterize such and such objects in such and such ways, we may do so for subjective reasons. There are numerous things which come under or are of the subjective kind. Let me mention some of them, (i) Human beings have this as a necessary constitution of their nature that when, for example, they are confronted with the case of that chief of a state telling that lie, they are bound to characterize it as morally shocking, (ii) Human beings, collectively or individually, have had this become a part of their unconscious nature in such a way that when they are confronted with that case, they irremediably characterize it as morally shocking, (iii) Human beings are so made by nature that when they are confronted with that case, they characterize it as morally shocking, (iv) Human beings, in this number or that, are so socially conditioned that when they are confronted with that case, they characterize it as morally shocking. (v) Human beings have their personal likes and dislikes. It belongs to their personal dislike that when they are confronted with that case they characterize it as morally shocking.

I have mentioned above five of the numerous sorts of things which are of the subjective kind. There should be no difficulty in seeing that the first two sorts of things are of the unavoidable variety. That is, they are such that, in case they are there, in being confronted with such and such objects, we cannot but characterize them in a subjective way. And thus, in case they are there, in being confronted with such and such objects, there is just no possibility of our characterizing them purely and simply on the basis of confrontation. Further, there should be no difficulty in seeing that the other three sorts of things are of the avoidable variety. That is, they are such that we can supersede them, although it would by no means be an easy thing to do. And, as a result, in being confronted with such and such objects, these three sorts of things need not stand in the way of our characterizing them purely and simply on the basis of confrontation.

I have mentioned above one kind of thing, that of the subjective kind, which falls under that something else, on account of which, and not on account purely and simply of confrontation, we may characterize such and such things in such and such ways. And I have mentioned above various sorts of things which are of the subjective kind; and I have said that some of them are of the unavoidable variety, and some of them avoidable. Now, we can go on to say that, whatever may fall under that something else, it would also be of the unavoidable or avoidable variety. And then we can go on to say about it, just as in respect of things of the subjective kind, the following: (1) if it is of the unavoidable variety, then, in case it is there, in our being confronted with such and such objects, we cannot but characterize them as mediated through it; and consequently we can never characterize them purely and simply as a result of confrontation; and (2) if it is of the avoidable variety, then we can supersede it, although possibly by no means in an easy manner; and consequently, in our being confronted with such and such objects, it need not stand in the way of our characterizing it purely and simply as a result of confrontation.

In the preceding I have raised the question: how do we know that, in being confronted with such and such objects, we are characterizing them in such and such ways, purely and simply on the basis of confrontation and not on the basis of something else? I have already answered this question above. In brief, the answer is this: (1) if that something else, whether of the subjective or some other kind, is of the unavoidable variety, then there is absolutely no possibility of our being able to characterize such and such objects in such and such ways purely and simply on the basis of confrontation; but (2) if it is of the avoidable variety, then we can supersede it, and consequently characterize such and such objects in such and such ways purely and simply on the basis of confrontation. Here I do not wish to deal with what all is required, what all the intellectual and moral work we need to put in, for this supersession.

V

Here let me state in short what I have tried to say in this paper, (1)1 have defined the notion of telling a lie, and distinguished it from several other notions (Section I). (2) I have said that, generally speaking, the notion of telling a lie is taken to belong to the moral realm. In this connection two things are said about it. Firstly, it is said that there is the moral law that one should not tell a lie. Secondly, it is said that there are exceptions to this law, just as there are exceptions to many other moral laws. I have profusely illustrated both these theses (Section II). (3) I have said that the moral role is not the only role which the notion of telling a lie plays in our life. It plays various other roles as well. I have mentioned some of them, and sufficiently illustrated them. I have said that a few of them give to the notion of telling a lie an additional respectability, that is, in addition to the respectability which it has by virtue of there being times when telling a lie is not of an immoral nature (Section III). (4) I have dealt with a problem which is not directly related to the notion of telling a lie, but which this notion enables us to discuss rather well. This problem is about how we know a moral law, say, the moral law, 'One should not tell a lie,' or the moral law, 'One should not tell a lie, except under conditions x.' I have maintained that although, being confronted with such and such cases, we call them moral or immoral (just as, being confronted with such and such cases, we call them red, or hot, or loud), we cannot always be sure that we are calling them so, purely and simply on the basis of confrontation; but there are times when we can be (Section IV).

14

Putting into Practice What One Professes

I

1. Four of Plato's Dialogues, *Euthyphro, Apology, Crito* and *Phaedo,* are concerned with the trial and death of Socrates.

In *Euthyphro,* Socrates meets Euthyphro in the Porch of King Archon and tells him that he has been charged by a young man called Meletus, whom he hardly knows and who 'has a beak, and long straight hair, and a beard which is ill grown',[1] with corrupting youth by denying old gods and inventing new ones. Euthyphro tells Socrates that he has himself been charged with impiety for prosecuting his father, who, as he says, has committed an unjust murder. This leads Socrates to engage Euthyphro in a discussion on the nature of piety. Euthyphro is made to advance one definition after another of piety, each of which in turn Socrates has no difficulty in showing as unsatisfactory. Euthyphro calls Socrates Daedalus who sets arguments in motion, makes them move and go round.

In *Apology,* Socrates is at his trial. He says that there are old charges against him, and there are new ones which Meletus has brought. He contends that hostility is the cause of these accusations. And, according to him, there are two causes of this hostility.

The first cause is this: Socrates narrates that Chaerephon, a one-time friend of his, once asked the oracle of Delphi whether there was anyone wiser than Socrates. And the oracle said that there was none. Socrates wondered at this, because he himself had no wisdom, great or small. He decided to meet men who were reputed to be wise, amongst politicians, poets and artisans, in order to verify the truth of what the oracle had said. And he found that they were not wise, although they thought that they were so. And he found that in this respect he was better off than they, because while, like them, he had no wisdom, unlike them, he did not think that he had wisdom. This exposure aroused hostility. But, Socrates says, 'I go about the world, obedient to the god, and search and make enquiry into the wisdom of anyone, whether citizen or stranger, who appears to be wise; and if he is not wise, then in vindication of the oracle I show him that he is not wise; and my occupation quite absorbs me, and I have no time to give to any public matter of interest or to any concern of mine, but I am in utter poverty by reason of devotion to the god'.[2]

The second cause of hostility is this: following the example of Socrates, many young men who came to him also started exposing men reputed to be wise. And this again aroused hostility against Socrates. '. . . Young men of the richer classes, who have not much to do, come about me of their own accord; they like to hear the pretenders examined, and they often imitate me, and proceed to examine others; there are plenty of persons, as they quickly discover, who think that they know something, but really know little or nothing; and then those who are examined by them instead of being angry with themselves are angry with me: This confounded Socrates, they say; this villainous misleader of youth!'[3]

Socrates observes that, not accusation, but envy and detraction would be the cause of his possible destruction, as they have been and would be the cause of destruction of many good men. However, he goes on to say that, with his reputation for wisdom, he was not going to demean himself and ask for mercy. He was also not going to ask for mercy, because it would be wrong to do so. In pursuance of his oath, the function of a judge is not to yield to entreaties, but to give judgement in accordance with the laws. If he did not do so, he would be guilty of perjury. Socrates would be doing something wrong in being a party to this situation. Socrates is sentenced to death.

In *Crito*, Crito visits Socrates in prison. He tells him that he had been allowed in at that early hour, because he knew the jailor and also had done him some kindness, and that he did not disturb him (Socrates) and waited, because, despite his impending death, he found him peacefully asleep. 'I have always thought you to be of a happy disposition; but never did I see anything like the easy, tranquil manner in which you bear the calamity.'[4]

Crito tells Socrates that he had come there to help him to escape. He tells him that he and the other friends of Socrates had enough money to arrange for his escape. He also mentions various reasons why he should escape. He says that, if he did not escape, (i) he would be playing into the hands of his enemies who wanted his destruction, (ii) he would be abdicating his responsibility towards his children, and (iii) he would be giving the people a chance to call his friends cowardly who did not help him to escape.

Socrates tells Crito that he would be guided by reason and reason alone, whatever the consequences. 'For I am and always have been one of those natures who must be guided by reason, whatever the reason may be which on reflection appears to me to be the best; and now that the chance has befallen me, I cannot repudiate my own words: the principle which I have hitherto honoured and revered I still honour, and unless we can find other and better principles, I am certain not to agree with you; no, not even if the power of the multitude could inflict many more imprisonments, confiscations, deaths, frightening us like children with hobgobling terrors.'[5]

Socrates mentions various things in reply to Crito's reasons for escaping, (i) In matters of body, the opinion of the one who knows and not of the many who do not know is to be followed;

so also in matters of soul, in matters of justice and injustice. 'Then, my friend, we must not regard what the many of us say; but what he, the one who has understanding of just, will say, and what the truth will say.'[6] (ii) One should never do evil, even as an act of retaliation.' . . . neither injury nor retaliation nor warding off evil by evil is ever right.'[7] (iii) If he escaped, he would be violating the laws which brought him into existence and nurtured and educated him and gave him a share in every good which they could provide. But, knowing what they were, if he still remained there, then he had entered into an implied contract with them that he would do what they said. And of all people, he had entered into an implied contract with them, because he had been the most constant resident of the city.'. . . the halt, the blind, the maimed were not more stationary. . .'[8] (iv) If he escaped, he would also be doing varied harm to his children, friends and himself. Socrates refuses to escape.

> 'This, dear Crito, is the voice which I seem to hear murmuring in my ears, like the sound of the flute in the ears of the mystic; that voice, I say, is humming in my ears, and prevents me from hearing any other. And I know that anything more which you say will be vain. Yet speak, if you have anything to say.
>
> *Crito*. I have nothing to say, Socrates.
>
> *Socrates*. Leave me then, Crito, to fulfil the will of God, and to follow whither he leads.'[9]

In *Phaedo*, Phaedo describes to Echecrates the last hours of Socrates' death. He tells him who were the people present, besides himself, at the time. He tells him that philosophy was discussed on the occasion, as it had been on the previous days also when they had met Socrates in prison. He reports to him on the various problems discussed. He mentions to him Socrates' argument why a philosopher is always willing to die. The argument is this: (1) death is the separation of soul and body; (2) philosopher aims at true knowledge, knowledge of true being, the essence of each thing, absolute justice, absolute good, absolute beauty, and so on; (3) this knowledge is possible only through thought or soul, unimpeded by body; (4) thus a philosopher is always willing to be with soul alone away from the body; and (5) thus a philosopher is always willing to die. Socrates goes on to say that it would be a ridiculous contradiction if philosophers were always willing to die and yet repining when death came. '. . . if they have been in every way the enemies of the body, and are wanting to be alone with the soul, when their desire is granted, how inconsistent would they be if they trembled and repined, instead of rejoicing at their departure to that place where, when they arrive, they hope to gain that which in life they desired—and this was wisdom—and at the same time to be rid of the company of their enemy.'[10]

Socrates dies by taking the cup of poison which is given to him.

I have given above a brief account of Plato's *Euthyphro*, *Apology*, *Crito* and *Phaedo*. I would like to abstract from it three of the things which Socrates professes there and which he also puts into practice. These are as follows: (1) on the basis of the reasons which he mentions, one should not ask for mercy; (2) on the basis of the various things which he mentions in reply to Crito's reasons for escaping, one should not escape; and (3) on the basis of the reasons which he mentions, a philosopher should be willing to die.

2. Now, suppose, after saying all that he does in favour of not asking for mercy, not escaping and a philosopher being willing to die, Socrates agrees to ask for mercy, agrees to escape and is unwilling to die. Then there is obviously an inconsistency between what he says and what he does, between his profession and his practice. As a result, that is, as a result of this inconsistency between what he says and what he does, we find that he becomes an object of our moral condemnation, we say that he has done something which he should not have done or has done something immoral. We morally expect or require that if he says what he does, then he will also act up to it. And if he does not do so, if he deviates from his profession, then we morally

condemn him. If we were to formulate the moral law underlying this attitude on our part, it would be 'One should put into practice what one professes'. This moral law is a (moral) way of bridging the gulf between what one professes and one's practice of it.

Now, take the following cases:

(1) Socrates does not put into practice what he professes, because in the course of time he finds himself lacking in those moral qualities which he needs in order to do so.

(2) Socrates does not put into practice what he professes, because in the meanwhile he finds better reasons for making some other profession which he then goes on to put into practice.

(3) Socrates professes whatever he professes. Consciously or unconsciously he may do so in order to present himself in a favourable light. But, of course, this does not mean that, while making his profession, he is not sure that he will put it into practice also. However, when the time comes, he is swayed by considerations of some personal gain and then he does not put it into practice. Socrates may go on to hide, if he can, that he has not put it into practice, or to rationalize his not doing so, or to become aggressive as a defence-mechanism about this.

In brief, Socrates does not put into practice what he professes, because he is swayed from doing so by considerations of some personal gain.

Let me go back to the second case first. It is not that Socrates does not put into practice what he professes. It is that he now finds better reasons to make a new profession in place of the old one which he then goes on to put into practice. As a result, in not putting into practice his earlier profession which he does not make any more, he is not an object of our moral condemnation. What may happen is that some people may consider his change of profession on the face of it a little intriguing or even suspect.

Let me go back to the first case next. Socrates, for example, advances a certain argument about why a philosopher should be willing to die. But, suppose that, as the time of death draws near, he is overtaken by what one may call the natural fear of death, which he is not able to conquer; and consequently in one way or another he would like to avoid being killed. We find that only an exceptional person is able to conquer this fear (and, we know, Plato does present Socrates as such an exceptional person). But suppose he is not able to conquer this fear. Then it seems to me that, while we may ridicule Socrates for his faith in the efficacy of his theory, we will find his conduct morally understandable or excusable, not morally condemnable.

Let me introduce a variation in the just-mentioned situation. Suppose that, as the time of his death draws near, Socrates is tempted to be able to continue to visit his usual haunts and engage with people in his familiar conversations, which (temptation) he is not able to resist; and consequently in one way or another he would like to avoid being killed. We find that people could normally be expected to resist this temptation, although indeed not without some difficulty. As a result, it seems to me that Socrates' conduct in the modified situation would be quite close to being morally condemnable.

Generally speaking, as far as the first case is concerned, we can say that a person's not putting into practice what he professes is sometimes morally condemnable and sometimes not. It is morally condemnable when he does not have the required moral qualities which people could normally be expected to have, although at times not without considerable difficulty. It is not morally condemnable when he does not have the required moral qualities which only an exceptional person could have. In this latter case his not putting into practice what he professes would be morally excusable.

Let me now go back to the third case. I find that, as in the first case, in the third case also, a person's not putting into practice what he professes is sometimes morally condemnable and sometimes not. It is morally condemnable when he is not able to resist his desire for personal gain which people could normally be expected to resist, although at times not without considerable difficulty, like the desire which Socrates may have to see his children settled before he dies. It is not morally condemnable when he is not able to resist his desire for personal gain which only an exceptional person could resist, like the desire which Socrates may have to see that his wife and children were not subjected to a fatal harm which he had good reasons to apprehend to take place when he was no more there. In this latter case a person's not putting into practice what he professes would be morally excusable, not morally condemnable.

I have mentioned above the moral law 'One should put into practice what one professes'. I have also mentioned above that a person's not putting into practice what he professes is morally excusable under certain specifiable circumstances. This makes us qualify or amend the given moral law in a certain way. The moral law would now be 'One should put into practice what one professes, it being morally excusable not to do so under certain specifiable circumstances.'

I would like to ask here: are there circumstances under which a person's not putting into practice what he professes is not just morally excusable but morally justified? For example, are there circumstances under which, although he professes that a philosopher should be willing to die, Socrates is morally justified in avoiding death?

Suppose a person has been falsely charged with some serious criminal offence, which also carries with it a grave penalty. And suppose that Socrates, and he alone, has in his possession evidence to the effect that this person has been falsely implicated. Then, it seems to me that, in case he cannot make this evidence available in some other way, Socrates would be morally justified in avoiding death for the required duration in order to save that person.

Somewhat generally speaking, we can say that Socrates is morally justified in avoiding death, in case a moral value or a higher moral value is at stake.

More generally speaking, we can say that a person is morally justified in not putting into practice what he professes, in case a moral value or a higher moral value is at stake.

This preceding consideration makes us further qualify or amend the moral law 'One should put into practice what one professes'. The moral law would now be 'One should put into practice what one professes, it being morally excusable or morally justified not to do so under certain specifiable circumstances'.

I may put together in this place some definitions.

(1) A person's not putting into practice what he professes is morally condemnatory, (i) if, in not doing so, no moral value or no higher moral value is at stake, or (ii) if, in doing so, no exceptional qualities, say, exceptional moral qualities, are required.

(2) A person's not putting into practice what he professes is morally excusable, if, in doing so, some exceptional qualities, say, exceptional moral qualities, are required.

(3) A person's not putting into practice what he professes is morally justified, if, in doing so, some moral value or some higher moral value is sought to be realized.

(4) A person's putting into practice what he professes is morally heroic, if, in doing so, some exceptional qualities, say, exceptional moral qualities, are required.

3. (1) Suppose, instead of professing any of the above-mentioned three things, Socrates professes 'One should escape and take revenge against people who have falsely charged him' or 'One should treat all non-Greeks as barbarians or uncivilized people'. Would one find his not putting into practice any of these two new professions also morally condemnatory, just as one finds his not putting into practice any of his other three professions morally condemnatory? Would one rather not have a sense of what I may call moral relief at his not putting them into practice as things which are morally wrong?

I have said above that a person's not putting into practice what he professes is not morally condemnatory but morally justified, if, in not doing so, some moral value or some higher moral value is sought to be realized. I take it as a negative part of this thesis that a person's not putting into practice what he professes is not morally condemnatory but morally justified, if, in not doing so, the realization of some negative moral value is sought to be avoided. As a result, Socrates' not putting into practice any of his two new professions is not morally condemnatory but morally justified, if they have a negative moral value. And we may say that we have a sense of moral relief at Socrates' not putting them into practice, if they have a negative moral value.

It may be noted here that it is not a part of my purpose in this place to contend whether or not any of Socrates' new professions really have a negative moral value, just as it was not a part of my purpose earlier to contend whether or not any of Socrates' other professions really had a positive moral value. A part of what I have done earlier is to mention various circumstances which make us qualify or amend the moral law 'One should put into practice what one professes'. One set of these circumstances are those under which a person's not putting into practice what he professes is not morally condemnatory but morally justified. I have now maintained that Socrates' not putting into practice any of his new professions, if they have a negative moral value, is a negative part of this thesis, that is, the thesis immediately preceding.

I have made use here of the notion of moral relief. For the time being, I understand this notion to be that of relief which one may have at a person's not putting into practice his profession which has a negative moral value. In contrast to this, I make use of the notion of immoral glee. And, for the time being again, I understand this notion to be that of glee which one may have at a person's putting into practice his profession which has a negative moral value.

(2) Plato presents Socrates as a man of wisdom, although his Socrates also never tires of saying that he has no wisdom. Now, suppose that Socrates, whom Plato presents as a man of

wisdom, professes that one should not escape. And then, suppose that somebody else who does not have wisdom in that sense, say, Crito, an ordinary human being like a large many of us, professes that one should not escape. I would like to ask here the question: why is it that we expect *more*, as, it seems to me, we do, from the former putting into practice what he professes than we do from the latter? And, in the negative case, why is it that we morally condemn *more*, as again, it seems to me, we do, the former not putting into practice what he professes than we do the latter?

We may take yet another example. Suppose that a man of wisdom professes that one should practise temperance. And then, suppose that somebody else who is not a man of wisdom in that sense professes the same thing. We may ask about this example the same questions as we have done about the other example.

I find that there are two reasons for our expecting *more* from a man of wisdom putting into practice what he professes than from somebody else. Firstly, we expect that a man of wisdom has given enough thought to what exactly he professes and to the implications of putting it into practice. Secondly, we expect somehow that he has the qualities, say, the moral qualities, to put into practice what he professes. Let me go back to my two examples. We expect that a man of wisdom has given enough thought to what exactly it means not to escape and to practise temperance, and to the fact that, possibly among other things, not escaping implies any amount of suffering for himself and very likely also for his kith and kin; and, again, possibly among other things, practising temperance implies an arduous task of resisting temptations. Further, we expect somehow that a man of wisdom, possibly among other things, is ready to put up with suffering for himself and for his kith and kin, and again possibly among other things, has it in him to resist temptations.

I have said that we expect more from a man of wisdom putting into practice what he professes than from somebody else. It is indeed a separate question whether he does indeed do so. And I am not going into it at present.

(3) Take the following cases:

(i) Suppose a person, who is a member of an institution, is deeply annoyed with some of the things which the authorities in that institution have been doing. And then, in a state of anger, he professes that one should not belong to such an institution.

(ii) Suppose a person wants something done at a public office. He finds that the man who is responsible for doing it does not pay any attention and continues to be busy with something else. The person concerned loses his temper and then there is a verbal encounter between the two sides, the work which was to be done remaining undone. After some time the person returns home and, in boastfulness, professes that one should teach such a man a lesson.

(iii) Suppose there is a set of people idling away and chatting and cursing other people. And then, while in that lighthearted mood, they profess that one should make a nuisance of oneself to such and such people.

Now, as regards the first case, we are inclined to say that the person has professed something in a state of anger; let one wait for a little while for things to cool down, and then he may take a different view of the matter. As regards the second case, especially if the person is a habitual boaster, we are inclined to say that he has professed something in boastfulness, and therefore he is not to be taken seriously. As regards the third case, we are inclined to say that the people have professed something in a mood of lightheartedness, and therefore, again, they are not to be taken seriously. That means to say that, in all these three cases (as also in many other cases), we are inclined to say that the people profess something only apparently, but not really. That is to say, they do not profess anything; they simply utter words to that effect.

We profess something when we do so after due thought. It is possible that, even while we are giving what we claim to be due thought, extraneous factors enter into our profession. When that happens, it is evidently essential to take note of them as soon as they are discovered, and say that we do not yet have a real profession. It is, of course, possible once more that, whether we profess something only apparently or really, there would be people who morally condemn us for not putting into practice what we profess.

4. I have mentioned above several examples in which we profess something in so many words. We may call this form of professing 'professing explicitly.' However, there is another form of professing also. In this form we profess something by living in a certain way. We may call this form of professing professing implicitly. And then, *mutatis mutandis*, we may go on to say about the latter various things which I have said about the former.

(i) The moral law: we should continue to live in the way in which we profess something by living in that way.

(ii) A person's not continuing to live in the way in which he professes something by living in that way is morally condemnatory, (a) if, in not continuing to live in that way, no moral value or no higher moral value is at stake, or (b) if, in continuing to live in that way, no exceptional qualities, say, exceptional moral qualities, are required.

(iii) A person's not continuing to live in the way in which he professes something by living in that way is morally excusable, if, in continuing to live in that way, some exceptional qualities, say, exceptional moral qualities, are required.

(iv) A person's not continuing to live in the way in which he professes something by living in that way is morally justified, if, in not continuing to live in that way, some moral value or some higher moral value is sought to be realized, or negatively, the realization of some negative moral value is sought to be avoided.

(v) A person's continuing to live in the way in which he professes something by living in that way is morally excusable, if, in continuing to live in that way some exceptional qualities, say, exceptional moral qualities, are required.

(vi) As I understand that term for the time being, moral relief is a relief which one may have at a person's not continuing to live in the way in which one professes something by living in that way which has a negative moral value.

(vii) Again, as I understand that term for the time being, immoral glee is glee which one may have at a person's continuing to live in the way in which he professes something by continuing to live in that way which has a negative moral value.

5. Let me state briefly what I have tried to say in part I of this paper.

(a) I have said that we morally condemn a person for not putting into practice what he professes. And I have mentioned the moral law 'One should put into practice what one professes'. And then, I have mentioned the circumstances when a person's not putting into practice what he professes is not morally condemnatory, but morally excusable or morally justified.

(b) I have argued that we morally expect *more* from a man of wisdom putting into practice what he professes than from somebody else. And, likewise, we morally condemn *more* a man of wisdom not putting into practice what he professes than somebody else.

(c) I have mentioned several cases where a person does not really profess; he only uses words to that effect. And I have mentioned when it is that a person does really profess.

(d) I have distinguished between 'professing explicitly' and 'professing implicitly'.

(e) In the course of these various deliberations, I have defined the expressions: (i) morally condemnatory, (ii) morally excusable, (iii) morally justified, (iv) morally heroic, (v) moral relief, and (vi) immoral glee.

II

1. There is a continuing and widely prevalent belief that when one puts into practice what one professes, what it means is that, for example, Socrates professes that one should not ask for mercy in his situation and he does not do so, one should not escape in his situation and he does not do so, and a philosopher should be willing to die and he is willing to do so. In other words, when one puts into practice what one professes, what it means is that there is a straightforward conformity between what one professes and one's putting it into practice.

I would like to ask here the following two questions:

(a) Is it the case that when one puts into practice what one professes there need not always be a straightforward conformity between what one professes and one's putting it into practice, but this does not mean that there is no conformity between them? Differently expressed, is it the case that when one puts into practice what one professes, there need not always be a conformity in word between what one professes and one's putting it into practice, but this does not mean that there is no conformity in spirit between them?

(b) Is it the case that when one puts into practice what one professes, there is sometimes conformity in word between what one professes and one's putting it into practice, but there is no conformity in spirit between them?

2. In the preceding section I have used: (1) the notion of straightforward conformity or conformity in word between what one professes and one's putting it in to practice; and (2) the notion of conformity in spirit between what one professes and

one's putting it into practice. I would now like to determine the nature of these two notions.

Firstly, let me determine the nature of the former notion. This is done relatively easily. I have already mentioned above some examples of this notion. On the basis of these examples, we can say that we have conformity in word when what we put into practice is a mirror-image or replica, so to say, of what we profess. We profess something and then it is reproduced, so to say, in practice. I may mention here a couple of other examples of this notion: one professes that, in keeping with the Hindu system of organization of life into different stages, one should renounce the world at such and such age, and one renounces the world at such and such age; and one professes that, in keeping with the Gandhian scheme of basic education, one should send one's children to a basic education school, and one sends one's children to a basic education school.

This brings me to determine the nature of conformity in spirit.

Suppose one professes that the people should try to resolve conflicts of opinion among themselves through discussion.

Let me take the following cases in this connection:

(1) The persons A and B are engaged in discussion about whether all human beings should have certain basic rights. A is of the view that they should. According to him, their possession of these basic rights will enable them to develop in their own peculiar way, thus contributing enormously to the richness of humanity; and it will also protect them against exploitation. On the other hand, B is of the view that their possession of these basic rights will make them selfish; and even when they co-exist, they will be doing so for selfish reasons. He suggests that, instead of certain basic rights, all human beings should have certain basic concerns (for others), like some physical and mental care of other people. According to him, their possession of these basic concerns, needless to say, will contribute enormously to general

human welfare; and, concerns as these are for others, there will also be no question of exploitation. A and B go on to argue in this way, until A is able to convince B, or *vice versa*, or both agree to disagree at least for the time being.

(2) The persons A and B are engaged in discussion about whether women constitute a specially suppressed class of people. A is of the view that they do. On the other hand, B is of the view that there are suppressed people among men, and there are suppressed people among women. And if we are looking for a specially suppressed class (or classes) of people, then we will not find it to consist of men merely or of women merely, but of both. And in relation to this specially suppressed class of people, we will find the suppressors among both men and women. A may continue to hold the view that women do constitute a specially suppressed class of people (while not denying that there may be other specially suppressed classes of people). And he may go on to support his contention by mentioning how throughout the ages and throughout the world, by virtue of being the weaker sex, they have been singled out for specially harsh treatment. A may go on and on in this way, giving B no further chance even to get a word in edgeways. B keeps listening to what A has been saying, trying to draw from it its quintessence, and deciding to consider it on his own most carefully.

(3) The persons A and B are engaged in discussion about whether young men and women in an educational institution should have complete freedom in respect of the sexual life which they would like to lead. A is of the view that they should. According to him, they should have complete freedom to do with their own lives what they want. On the other hand, B is of the view that if these young men and women are members of a relatively conservative society, then their having the

complete freedom under consideration, at least at one go, would be a cause of a great turmoil in that society. And, further, even in a society which is rather liberal, one should not be entirely neglectful of the various consequences of this freedom. A is furious at B's argumentation, and charges him with being an obscurantist, an enemy of liberalism. B chooses to be silent at A's outburst.

(4) The persons A and B together are involved in a controversy over something with the authorities with or under whom they work. The authorities are of the view that the controversy can only be resolved in manner m. A and B are of the view that this controversy can only be resolved in manner n. Now, as the deliberations proceed, B finds himself in a position to suggest that the controversy could perhaps also be resolved in manner o, o being some kind of a compromise position between m and n. While the authorities, after some hesitation, accept this new way of resolving the controversy, A feels let down by B for not having stuck to n in their joint opposition to the authorities. B may want to discuss with A whether he was justified in suggesting o as a means of resolving the controversy between them and the authorities, but the sense of hurt of A prevents him from reciprocating B's desire. Every move which B may make in the direction of discussion may indeed be met with a look of cold contempt by A. Now, in relation to A's attitude of not being prepared to discuss out of anger, B decides to wait, hoping that in the course of time A will eventually cool down and come round.

Now, take these four cases which I have mentioned in connection with the profession that people should try to resolve conflicts of opinion among themselves through discussion. In the first case, the discussion has the form which it would have if it conformed to its form in word. This does not, however, mean that it may not conform to this form in spirit as well. In the second case, one comes to a point where one adopts the attitude of listening to what is being said, and then considering it on one's own most carefully. In the third case, again, one comes to a point where one adopts the attitude of being silent. In the fourth case, once again, one comes to a point where one adopts the attitude of waiting and hoping that things will turn out all right in the course of time. Here it is evident that, in the latter three cases, the discussion does not have the form which it would have if it conformed to its form in word. But I take it that, in all these cases, it still does have some or the other form which it could have under the circumstances, the form of ultimately listening to what is being said and considering it on one's own most carefully, the form of ultimately being silent, and the form of ultimately waiting and hoping that things will turn out all right in the course of time.

We could say that our putting into practice what we profess would conform to what we profess in spirit, if it involves, firstly, our looking for the (inner) meaning of what we profess, secondly, our seeing what (outer) form it could take under the circumstances keeping in view its (inner) meaning, and, thirdly, our giving it that form. It could have, as in the above-mentioned first case, the form which it would have if it conformed to its form in word; or it could have, as in the other three above-mentioned cases, some other form. Evidently, in the former case, its form in spirit would coincide with its form in word; in the latter three cases, its form in spirit would be different from its form in word.

3. Let me now return to the two questions which I have asked in section one of this part of the paper. These questions, somewhat differently and in the case of the first question somewhat briefly stated, are: (1) may it not happen that our putting into practice what we profess does not sometimes conform to what we profess in word, but it does so in spirit? and (2) may it not happen that

our putting into practice what we profess sometimes conforms to what we profess in word, but it does not do so in spirit?

In section two of this part of the paper, I have tried to determine the nature of the notion of our putting into practice what we profess in word, and that of the notion of our putting into practice what we profess in spirit. And in connection with our doing the latter, I have talked of the possibility of our putting into practice what we profess in spirit coinciding with our putting into practice what we profess in word, and the possibility of our putting into practice what we profess in spirit not coinciding with our putting into practice what we profess in word.

In all, in connection with our putting into practice what we profess, there is the question concerning four possibilities:

(i) concerning the possibility of our putting into practice what we profess in word being there, and our putting into practice what we profess in spirit also being there;
(ii) concerning the possibility of our putting into practice what we profess in word being there, but our putting into practice what we profess in spirit not being there;
(iii) concerning the possibility of our putting into practice what we profess in spirit being there, but our putting into practice what we profess in word not being there; and
(iv) concerning the possibility of neither our putting into practice what we profess in word being there nor our putting into practice what we profess in spirit being there.

Now, in order to deal with the question concerning these four possibilities, let me revert to the profession that people should try to resolve conflicts of opinion among themselves through discussion. And let me suppose that the (inner) meaning of this profession is that people should try to resolve conflicts of opinion among themselves through an interchange of ideas with a view to attaining truth. Then it is possible that all this happens, and there is also the form which there would be if there was conformity in word, that is to say that it is possible that our putting into practice what we profess conforms to what we profess in spirit as well as in word. This would be our answer to the question concerning the above-mentioned first possibility. Further, it is possible that, in people's trying to resolve conflicts of opinion among themselves, there is a certain interchange of ideas with a view to attaining truth, or there is an attempt at such an interchange; but, on account of the circumstances which are there, there is not the form which there would be if there was conformity in word, but there is some other form instead. That is to say that our putting into practice what we profess, in some way conforms to what we profess in spirit but not in word. This would be our answer to the question concerning the above-mentioned third possibility.

It may have been noted that both these possibilities have already been indicated above, the former possibility in respect of the first case mentioned in section two of this part of the paper and the latter possibility in respect of the other three cases mentioned there.

Still further, we find there to be the following two things: (a) there are occasions when, out of fatigue or boredom or lack of real interest or desire to keep up appearances, in trying to resolve conflicts of opinion among themselves, people go through all the motions of a discussion, there are questions and answers, there is the form which there would be if there was conformity in word. But, as far as one can see, there is no interchange of ideas with a view to attaining truth. That is to say that there are occasions when our putting into practice what we profess conforms to what we profess in word but not in spirit, (b) Likewise, there are occasions when, again for the same reasons as those just-mentioned, in trying to resolve conflicts of opinion among themselves, people go through all the motions of a discussion which they might do under some special circumstances, claiming to listen and consider on one's own later on or claiming to be silent or claiming to wait and hope for things to turn out all right. But once more, as far as one can see, there is no interchange of ideas or there is no attempt at such an interchange, with a view to attaining truth. That is to say that there are occasions when our putting into practice what we profess does not conform to what we profess either in word or in spirit. These two things are our answers to the question concerning the above-mentioned second and fourth possibility, respectively.

The answers which I have given here to the question concerning the four possibilities mentioned above, contain the answers to the two questions which I have mentioned in section one of this part of the paper and which I have repeated in the beginning of the present section. The answers are that our putting into practice what we profess may conform to what we profess in spirit but not in word, or it may conform to it in word but not in spirit. This shows that the continuing and widely prevalent belief that I have mentioned in the beginning of the first section, namely the view that our putting into practice what we profess means straightforward conformity to what we profess or conformity to what we profess in word, this view is not justified.

Let me state in brief what I have tried to say in part II of this paper.

(1) I have mentioned the continuing and widely prevalent belief that our putting into practice what we profess means its straightforward conformity to what we profess or its conformity to what we profess in word.

(2) I have posed two questions concerning this belief, namely the question concerning the possibility of our putting into practice what we profess conforming to what we profess in spirit but not in word, and that of the possibility of its conforming to it in word but not in spirit.

(3) I have tried to determine the nature of the notion of our putting into practice what we profess conforming to what we profess in word and that of conforming to it in spirit.

(4) As a part of showing various possibilities concerning our putting into practice what we profess conforming to what we profess in word or its conforming to it in spirit,

I have tried to show that it is possible for it to conform to it in spirit but not in word, or to conform to it in word but not in spirit. And that means that the above-mentioned continuing and widely prevalent belief is not justified.

Notes

1. *The Dialogues of Plato*, translated by B. Jowett, Random House, Vol. I, p. 383.
2. *Ibid.*, Vol. I, p. 406.
3. *Ibid.*, Vol. I, p. 406.
4. *Ibid.*, Vol. I, p. 427.
5. *Ibid.*, Vol. I, p. 430.
6. *Ibid.*, Vol. I, p. 431.
7. *Ibid.*, Vol. I, p. 433.
8. *Ibid.*, Vol. I, p. 436.
9. *Ibid.*, Vol. I, p. 438.
10. *Ibid.*, Vol. I, p. 451.

15

Moral Exceptions

I

Kant conceives of a moral law as a categorical imperative. One, and possibly the most well-known, way, in which he expresses the latter is: 'Act only on that maxim through which you can at the same time will that it should become a universal law.'[1] One of the major criticisms which has long been made against this formulation of a categorical imperative is that it would make a moral law too rigorous. And the reason which has been advanced for this formulation making a moral law too rigorous is that it does not allow exceptions to a moral law, whereas there are exceptions to at least many a moral law. The example which is most frequently mentioned in this connection is that of the moral law about speaking the truth and there being exceptions to it, as when protecting the life of an innocent person who was being pursued by a murderer and who had taken refuge with us. In his essay, 'On an Alleged Right to Lie from the Motive of Benevolence,'[2] Kant himself mentions this criticism, and this reason for which it is made and the very same example which is most frequently put forward in the matter, as he finds all that in Benjamin Constant's work, *France,* 1797, Part Six, No. 1: On Political Reactions, pages 123–4; and then he also goes on to discuss what Constant has to say. I will state here what Constant has to say as well as Kant's consideration of it.

As Kant presents it and as I understand it, concerning the criticism of rigorousness against Kant's above-mentioned formulation of a categorical imperative and the reason for which it is made and making use of the very same example which is most frequently put forward in the matter, Constant says two things: (1) the moral law that it is one's duty to speak the truth, when taken as unconditional and in isolation, would make society impossible. This is proved by Kant's drawing from it the consequence that it would be a crime to tell a lie to a murderer, who was after our friend and who had taken refuge with us. 'The moral principle that it is duty to speak the truth, if one took it as unconditional and in isolation, would make society impossible. We have the proof of this in the very immediate consequence which is drawn from this principle by a German philosopher, who goes so far as to maintain that it would be a crime to tell a lie to a murderer, who asked us whether our friend, whom he was pursuing, had taken refuge in our house.'[3] (2) Duties and rights are correlative; thus the person A's duty to speak the truth is correlative with the person B's right to have the truth spoken to him; but B does not have the right to have the truth spoken to him, if speaking the truth to him harms somebody else; hence A does not have a duty to speak the truth to B, if speaking the truth to B harms somebody else. In brief, A's duty to speak the truth is qualified by B's right to have the truth spoken to him. 'It is a duty to speak the truth. The concept of duty is inseparable from the concept of right. A duty is which in one being corresponds with a right in another. Where there is no right, there is no duty. Thus it is a duty to speak the truth, but only to one who has a right to the truth. But no one has a right to a truth, which harms another.'[4]

Now, again as I see it, in discussing what Constant has to say, Kant also says two things: (1) he distinguishes between truth and truthfulness. By the former notion, I understand him to mean that which one says is true or happens to be true; and by the latter notion, I understand him to mean one's speaking the truth as one knows or believes it to be. According to him, it makes no sense to talk of one's right to truth, because that would make truth dependent on one's will. One can only talk of one's right to one's own truthfulness. '... the expression that one has a right to truth is one without meaning. We should rather say that one has a right to one's own truthfulness (*veracitas*), i.e. to subjective truth in one's person. For objectively having a right to truth would be so much as to say, as with Mine and Thine generally, that it depends upon one's will whether a given proposition should be true or false ...'[5] (2) Apparently referring to the example where there is the question of telling a lie to the murderer concerned, Kant raises the question whether it is one's duty to be untruthful in statements to which one is unjustly forced, in order to protect somebody against a threatened crime. And he contends that: (i) it is one's formal duty towards others to be truthful in statements which one cannot avoid, however disadvantageous that may happen to be to anyone; and (ii) although, in being untruthful towards the person who unjustly forces one to make a statement, one does him no wrong, yet one does wrong to humanity in general, insofar as, as far as it lies in one's power, one does something as a result of which, generally speaking, statements, including those made in a contract, lose their credibility. 'Truthfulness in statements, which one cannot avoid, is one's formal duty towards others, however great a disadvantage may result from it to one's own self or to somebody else; and although I do not do any wrong to him who unjustly forces me to make a statement in falsifying it, I do indeed do wrong, through this falsification which can be called a lie (even though not in the legal sense), to duty in general in the most essential point; that is, so far as it lies in me, I bring this about that statements (declarations) generally do not find any credibility, and consequently all rights which are grounded in contracts also become void and lose their force; which is a wrong inflicted upon humanity in general.'[6]

It will be seen here that Kant's second point relates to Constant's first point, and his first point relates to the latter's second point.

Now, for the time being, I would only like to make one comment on Constant's first point and two main comments on Kant's second point.

(1) It is not clear why Constant maintains that society would become impossible as a result of Kant's conceiving the moral law about speaking the truth as being unconditional, and consequently not allowing the person concerned to tell a lie to the murderer concerned. What would become impossible is the kind of society which Constant may have in mind, namely the society in which it is the moral duty of the person concerned to tell a lie to the murderer concerned. It seems to me that what Constant really wants to say here is simply that there is something morally not quite all right in the person concerned not telling a lie to the murderer concerned. There is just no need to refer to the idea of society in this place. And if this is the case, then what we have before us at present is, on the one hand, the thesis, which Constant attributes to Kant, about the moral law about speaking the truth as being unconditional, and, on the other hand, Constant's thesis about there being conditions under which a person would be morally justified in telling a lie.

(2) As regards the first sub-point of Kant's second point, on the basis of what he says there, it follows that he rejects Constant's contention about it being the moral duty of the person concerned to tell a lie to the murderer concerned, and consequently the latter's implied contention of there being exceptions to the thesis, which Constant attributes to Kant, about the moral law about speaking the truth as being unconditional, and one of Kant's rejections of Constant's criticisms of this thesis.

(3) As regards the second sub-point of Kant's second point, on the basis of what he says there, the moral law about speaking the truth would be converted into a conditional or hypothetical law, i.e. a law which depends for its validity on its embodying or articulating the instrumentality of producing such and such consequences, here the consequence of the person concerned not contributing to the statements losing their credibility and consequently not doing wrong to humanity in general. And this

would be incompatible with his above-mentioned formulation of a categorical imperative which demands universality or unconditionality of a moral law. Here it may be mentioned in passing that if Kant maintains that, in telling a lie to the murderer concerned, the person concerned contributes to the statements losing their credibility and thus he does wrong to humanity in general; then it can be maintained with no less plausibility that, in telling a lie to the murderer concerned, the person concerned contributes to the assurances losing their credibility and thus he does wrong to humanity in general. But, as a matter of fact, here, in telling a lie to the murderer concerned, the person concerned need not be contributing to the statements losing their credibility; for it may be said to be understood that he is not telling a lie just like that, but on account of his belief that his doing so under the circumstances overrules the claims of speaking the truth. There is indeed the possibility that he speaks the truth, but then he should be prepared even to stake his life towards keeping his assurance.

Now, I have already left out from commenting Constant's second point and Kant's first point. We may also leave out the second sub-point of Kant's second point for the reason that it is incompatible with his above-mentioned formulation of a categorical imperative, which is his conception of a moral law. As a result, from what Constant has said and what Kant has said about this and what I have said about both, what we have before us is as follows: (1) Kant's affirmation that the moral law about speaking the truth is unconditional, and consequently his rejection of Constant's contention that there are exceptions to this law; and (2) Constant's contention that there are exceptions to this law.

As things stand at present, they are the same as I stated them in the beginning of this paper. In terms of Kant's above-mentioned formulation of a categorical imperative, we have his thesis that a moral law is universal or unconditional. And we have the criticism of this thesis that it makes a moral law too rigorous, because it does not allow exceptions to it.

II

1. The moral law which is most frequently mentioned as the law to which there are exceptions is the moral law that one should speak the truth. And likewise the example of exception which is most frequently mentioned is almost the same which Constant mentions, namely that of telling a lie in order to protect the life of an innocent person who was being pursued by a murderer and who had taken refuge with us. There is a slight variation of this example in the *Mahabharata*. I take this example as I find it in Herbert Herring's *Essentials of Kant's Theoretical and Practical Philosophy.*[7] In the *Mahabharata*, Kaushika, who was called *Satyavadin* because he had taken the vow to always speak the truth, sees some travellers, who were being pursued by robbers, take shelter near his cottage. The robbers come and ask Kaushika whether he had seen the travellers, and if so, where they were. Now, although being aware of what the robbers wanted, in keeping with his vow to always speak the truth, he tells them that he had seen the travellers and where they were. And then, of course, the robbers go on to do their job. In the *Mahabharata*, Kaushika is condemned for not telling a lie under the circumstances. There Krishna mentions this example to Arjuna 'in order to drive home the point that merely sticking to the vow for the sake of it, without serving the intent of the vow, would not only be a folly but even immoral.'[8] Let me mention here just one more example of an exception which is not without similarity with the preceding two examples. Somebody is seriously ill. Somebody else who claims to be his well-wisher, makes it a point to visit him frequently, makes himself comfortable by his bedside and engages himself in an endless chit-chat with him. All this, needless to say, causes the patient great strain and much harm. The people tell the visitor politely and then even bluntly that the patient needs rest and the visits cause him great strain and much harm. But the visitor refuses to pay any attention, believing that he is really entertaining the patient and drawing him out of his present gloomy state. And

then the people are left with no alternative but to tell the visitor a lie that the doctors have strictly forbidden all visits to the patient.

2. Let me take another moral law and exceptions to it. The law is: 'One should put into practice what one professes.' I have arrived at this law in the following manner: in Plato's *Apology*, where Socrates is on trial, Socrates mentions several reasons why he would not ask for mercy. In Plato's *Crito*, where Crito tries to persuade Socrates to escape from prison, Socrates mentions various reasons why he would not escape. In Plato's *Phaedo*, where Socrates is waiting to die, Socrates mentions an argument why a philosopher is willing to die. Now, suppose that after saying all that, Socrates is prepared to ask for mercy, is prepared to escape, and is unwilling to die. Then there is obviously an inconsistency between what he says and what he does, between his profession and practice. As a result, that is, as a result of this inconsistency between what he says and what he does, we find that he becomes a subject of our moral condemnation, we say that he has done something which he should not have done or has done something immoral. We morally expect or require that if he says what he does, then he will also act up to it. And if he does not do so, if he deviates from his profession; then we morally condemn him. The above-mentioned moral law is only an articulation of this attitude on our part.

Now, in order to see exceptions to the moral law which I have mentioned in the preceding paragraph, let me take a specific instance of this law. The specific instance is that if Socrates professes, as he does on the basis of a certain argument, that a philosopher is willing to die, then with his own commitment to philosophy he should be willing to die. I will presently mention two exceptions to this specific instance. (1) Suppose that, as the time of his death draws near, Socrates is overtaken by what one might call the awesome natural fear of death, which he is not able to conquer, and consequently in one way or another he would like to avoid being killed. Then I am inclined to think that Socrates's unwillingness to die under the present circumstances, and not, say, under the circumstance that he would like to live in order to be able to visit his usual haunts and engage with people in his familiar conversations, would not be morally condemnatory but morally excusable. (2) Suppose a person has been falsely charged with some serious criminal offence, which also carries with it a grave penalty. And suppose that Socrates, and he alone, has in his possession evidence to the effect that this person has been falsely implicated. Then it seems to me that, in case he cannot make this evidence available in some other way, Socrates would be morally justified in avoiding death for the required duration in order to save that person.

3. Let me mention yet another moral law and exceptions to it. This is the well-known moral law that one should not break or go back on one's word or promise. I will presently mention two exceptions to it, just as in the previous case. (1) Suppose the following to be the case: there is a person who has gone underground resisting a dictatorial regime. There is another person, say, a young girl, who has undertaken to function as a contact between him and the world outside; she takes messages from him and communicates them to the world outside, and takes messages from the world outside and communicates them to him. However, time comes when the police are able to lay their hands on her. And then she is tortured to find out where the resister was. And when that does not succeed, the members of her family, her parents, her brothers and sisters, and her other dear ones, are tortured in front of her. And then it is found that she cannot take that any more and lets the police know where the resister was. Here I am inclined to think that the young girl's going back on her assurance under the present circumstance, and not, say, under the circumstance that she was in some way lured by the police to tell them where the resister was, would not be morally blameworthy but morally excusable. (2) Again suppose the following to be the case: say, through her own conversations with him and through other people who may also have had conversations with him, the young girl has a firm indication that the resister has some deep personal grudge against the

person who is in the seat of power, and as a result what he really wants is not so much to fight the dictatorial regime as to remove that other person from his seat of power or to do away with him. As a matter of fact, he would not even mind occupying the seat of power himself, endowed with the same dictatorial powers. Then it seems to me that the young girl would not only be morally justified in withdrawing her assurance, she may also be morally justified in going back on it and accordingly informing the police about the whereabouts of the resister towards preventing a future possible danger from taking place.

4. Let me mention just one more moral law and exceptions to it. This moral law, which many recognize it to be so, is that one should not inflict pain or death on a living being. Once more I would presently mention two exceptions to it. (1) Suppose there is an animal, say, a dog, who is suffering from some incurable disease, which it is a sheer agony to bear or which has put him into a coma. Then it seems to me that one would be morally justified in putting an end to his life in his own interest. Here the question may be asked whether one would also be morally justified in putting an end to the life of a human being in his own interest, when he was likewise suffering from some incurable disease, which it was a sheer agony to bear or which had put him into a coma? I cannot help answering this question in the affirmative as well, in the interest of consistency. But I would like to add one qualification in this case. The qualification is that, if the person has not been put into coma, then one should take his explicit approval before putting an end to his life. (2) Suppose there is an animal, say, a man-eater, or there is even a human being, say, an insane human killer, who is going around killing people and other living beings; and suppose there is no other way of bringing him under control; then it seems to me that one would be morally justified in putting an end to his life for the protection of one's own self as of others.[9]

I have mentioned above four moral laws and some of the exceptions to them. I need not mention any more of these laws and any of the exceptions to them. Although it is not a part of my present work, I may mention here in passing some of those laws which do not seem to me to have any exceptions to them. These laws include the following: 'A person who has been asked to adjudicate should do so impartially'; 'One should not take advantage of somebody's helpless position'; 'One should not make use of one's superior position, physically or socially or economically or in some other way, to take advantage of somebody or to humiliate him or to destroy him or something else of that sort'; and 'One should treat all living beings, *qua* living beings, as equal.'

III

In the first section above, I have mainly mentioned Kant's thesis that a moral law is a universally valid law; and the widespread criticism of this thesis that it is too rigorous in character, because there are exceptions to at least many a moral law, as, for example, there are exceptions to the moral law that one should speak the truth. In the second section above, I have not merely mentioned once more the moral law that one should speak the truth and even further exceptions to it than what is mentioned in the first section, I have also mentioned some more moral laws and exceptions to them. Here the question will naturally be asked whether I then support the criticism that Kant's thesis that a moral law is a universally valid law is too rigorous in character, that, in other words, a moral law is not a universally valid law. I see at present two alternatives to my answering this question in the affirmative. One of the alternatives is this: Kant may be right in maintaining that a moral law is a universally valid law, but the examples of moral laws which one may be mentioning, even the examples of moral laws which Kant may himself be mentioning, are not examples of genuine moral laws. The other alternative is this: again Kant may be right in maintaining that a moral law is a universally valid law, and there are evidently no exceptions to the examples of moral laws which one may be mentioning, or those which Kant may himself be mentioning, when they are properly reformulated.

Now, as far as the first alternative is concerned, while conceding that Kant may be right in maintaining that a moral law is a universally valid law, 1 do not deny that the examples of moral laws which one may be mentioning, or those which Kant may himself be mentioning, may not be examples of genuine moral laws. And, as far as the second alternative is concerned, Kant may be right in maintaining that a moral law is a universally valid law, and I find it to be the case that there are evidently no exceptions to the examples of moral laws which one may be mentioning, or which Kant may himself be mentioning, when they are properly reformulated. Let me explain the point made in the latter part of this statement. And let me once more take the example of the moral law that one should speak the truth for the purpose. What is not infrequently held is that there is the moral law 'One should speak the truth', but there are circumstances, like protecting an innocent person's life or property or guarding somebody's well-being, when one would be morally justified in telling a lie, that is, there are exceptions to the given moral law. What I find to be the case is this: suppose there are exceptions to the given moral law, like the ones just mentioned, and suppose these are the only exceptions to it, then one can reformulate the moral law about speaking the truth as 'One should speak the truth, except under such and such specified circumstances' (rather than simply formulate it as 'One should speak the truth'). It will be noticed that, in the reformulated moral law, the excepting circumstances are not external to it (as they would be on the other formulation) but are its internal elements. And to this reformulated moral law there are evidently no exceptions. What I have said here about the moral law that one should speak the truth may be said about other moral laws as well to which there are said to be exceptions. The general form of all these moral laws when reformulated would be 'One should follow the given moral law m, except under the circumstances c.'

It would be illuminating to mention here a certain controversy between Paton and Moore. In his article, 'The Alleged

Independence of Good,' which he contributed to the volume on *The Philosophy of G.E. Moore*,[10] Paton contends that the (moral) goodness of some of the actions is dependent upon circumstances. In this connection he gives the example of Sir Philip Sidney, who in dying resigned to a wounded soldier the cup of water which had been offered him. And he concludes from this that Sir Philip's action was good under these circumstances, while it would not be good (or as good) if he had been well.[11] Moore's correct and notable answer to this objection is this. It is not the case that the action 'a_1' is good under circumstances x, y, z, and the same action 'a_1' is bad under circumstances x_1, y_1 z_1, In reality, there are at present two different actions, the whole of the action 'a_1 under x, y, z' and the whole of the action 'a_1 under x_1, y_1, z_1' where x, y, z and x_1, y_1, z_1 do not signify two different sets of circumstances under which one and the same action 'a_1' occurs, but essential qualities of two different actions. And what is good is the whole of 'the action a, under x, y, z' (not the action 'a_1' under x, y, z), and what is not good (or not so good) is the whole of 'the action a, under x_1, y_1, z_1' (not the action 'a_1' under x_1, y_1, z_1).[12]

One can express what I have said above differently also, and possibly more neatly. I have said above that given, say, the moral law that one should speak the truth, in respect of which there are circumstances,—like protecting the life of an innocent person who is being pursued by a murderer and who has taken refuge with us, or protecting the life or property of those whom somebody wants to harm, or protecting the well-being of somebody against encroachments,—in which one would be morally justified in telling a lie, that is, in respect of which there are exceptions; we can reformulate the moral law in such a way that these exceptions are accommodated within that law itself, and then to this reformulated moral law there are no exceptions. The other way of expressing it is this: again given, say, the moral law that one should speak the truth, in respect of which there are the said exceptions, what is happening is that there is the moral law that one should speak the truth, and there is, say, the moral law that one should protect the life of an innocent person who is being pursued by a murderer and who has taken refuge with us, which is higher than the former, and which, as a result, in a situation of conflict between them, supersedes it. Here it is not the case that the former moral law is not universally valid. What is the case is that both the moral laws are equally universally valid, but the latter is higher than the former, and which, as a result, in a situation of conflict between them, supersedes it. In fact, by implication, one may go on to add in this place, if, in a situation of conflict between them, one follows the lower moral law, then one does what is wrong; just as, in the earlier mode of expressing things, one does what is wrong in doing such and such in the face of its excepting circumstances.[13]

I have said above that given, say, the moral law that one should speak the truth, this moral law is superseded by, say, the moral law that one should protect the life of an innocent person who is being pursued by a murderer and who has taken refuge with us, which is higher than the former, in a situation of conflict between them. From the second and third examples of moral laws and exceptions to them which I have mentioned in the second section of this paper, it will be seen that there is yet another thing on account of which it would be morally in order to supersede or not to follow a given moral law. This thing is the non-possession by a person of some exceptional quality (qualities) which is required to follow that moral law, for example, the non-possession by a person of the exceptional quality of being able to suffer to the utmost extent towards keeping his assurance. Thus, as I find, there are two things on account of which it would be morally in order to supersede or not to follow a given moral law: the first thing is a higher moral law, in a situation of conflict between the two; and the second thing is the non-possession of some exceptional quality (qualities) which is required to follow a given moral law. We can say that, in the former case, one is morally justified in superseding or not following a given moral law; and, in the latter case, it would be morally excusable to supersede or not to follow a given moral law. These, as I find, are the two excepting circumstances in respect of the pursuit of a given moral law.

In the preceding paragraph, I have talked of an act being morally justified, or an act being morally excusable. I have also talked of these two kinds of acts in sub-sections two and three of section two of the present paper. For the purposes of this paper, let me explicitly define them as follows: an act is morally justified, if in it one follows a moral law; in case of conflict between two moral laws, one of which is higher, one follows the higher one; and in case of conflict between two moral laws, both of which are of equal rank, one follows either of them. And an act is morally excusable, if in it one does not follow a moral law on account of one's non-possession of some exceptional quality (qualities) which is required in following it.

IV

I may sum up in this place what I have tried to say in this paper. (1) I have mentioned Kant's thesis that a moral law is of the nature of a categorical imperative, and that one of the ways in which a categorical imperative may be expressed is in terms of its being universally valid. (Section 1) (2) I have mentioned the widespread criticism that a moral law is not a universally valid law, because there are exceptions to it, as, for example, there are exceptions to the moral law that one should speak the truth. In this connection I have referred to Constant and Kant's response to what Constant has to say. (Section 1) (3) Besides the moral law that one should speak the truth and exceptions to it, I have mentioned some other moral laws and exceptions to them. (Section 2) (4) However, I have not concluded from this that a moral law is not a universally valid law. On the other hand, I have reformulated a moral law in such a way that there are no exceptions to a moral law as so reformutated. I have gone on to express a moral law in yet another, and possibly neater, way. (Section 3) (5) I have mentioned two kinds of excepting circumstances to our following a moral law. (Section 3) (6) I have defined a morally justified act and a morally excusable act. (Section 3).

Notes

1. *The Moral Law or Kant's Groundwork of the Metaphysic of Morals*, translated by H.J. Paton, Hutchinson's University Library, 1951 reprint, p. 88.
2. 'Über ein vermeintes Recht, aus Menschenliebe zu lügen' in Kant's *Kleinere Schriften zu Geschichtsphilosophie, Ethik und Politik*, Felix Mciner Velag, 1959. Statements reproduced from this essay in the present article are in our own translation.
3. Kant's *Kleinere Schriften*, p. 201.
4. *Ibid.*
5. (1) Kant's *Kleinere Schriften*, p. 202.
   (2) Does it even make sense to talk of one's right to one's own truthfulness, that is, to one's speaking the truth as one knows or believes it to be? Should one not rather simply talk of one's duty to one's own truthfulness?
6. *Ibid.*
7. Ajanta Publications, 1993, chapter on 'Is there a Right to Lie from Altruistic Motives?', p. 109.
8. *Ibid.*
9. Gandhi would consider killing a living being morally in order, when it is unavoidable (i) for self-preservation (using insecticide), or (ii) for the protection of one's own self and that of others (killing wild beasts when they are a danger), or (3) in the interest of a living being itself (mercy-killing).
10. *The Library of Living Philosophers*, Vol. IV, edited by Paul Arthur Schilpp, Northwestern University, 1912.
11. *The Philosophy of G.E. Moore*, p. 126.
12. *The Philosophy of G.E. Moore*, pp. 618–20.
    In this connection, also see Hare's *The Language of Morals*, Oxford University Press, 1952, 3.6, pp. 52–3, where he says: 'The fact that exceptions are made to them (our principles) is a sign, not of any essential looseness, but of our desire to make them as rigorous as we can. For what we are doing in allowing classes of exceptions is to make the principle not looser, but more rigorous. Suppose we start off with a principle never to say what is false, but regard this principle as provisional, and recognize that there may be exceptions. Suppose, then, that we decide to make an exception in the case of lies

told in war-time to deceive the enemy. The rule has now become "never say what is false, except in war-time to deceive the enemy." This principle, once the exception has been made explicit and included in the wording of the principle, is not looser than it was before, but tighter. In one large class of cases, where previously the possibility of exceptions was left open and we had to decide for ourselves, the position is now regulated: the principle lays down that in these circumstances we may say what is false.' Words within brackets in this quotation are our own.

The statement in the main text concerning the controversy between Paton and Moore I have reproduced from my article, 'Kant's Groundwork of Morality,' published in *Studi Internazionali Di Filosofia,* Autumn 1971, p. 150. In the same article, in footnote 113, I have also quoted Hare's statement.

13. In his *Immanuel Kant's Moral Theory* (Cambridge University Press, 1989), in part III, section 12 where he discusses Kant's reply to Constant, referring to Kant's moral law about speaking the truth and Constant's contention about a person's being morally justified in not speaking the truth in order to save the life of an innocent person who has taken refuge with us, Sullivan maintains that it would be within Kant's own theory to hold: (i) what we have here are two moral rules, the moral rule about speaking the truth, and the moral rule about being benevolent, in conflict; and (ii) if one did not follow the moral rule with a stronger obligation, in this case the moral rule about being benevolent, then one would be doing something which is not morally right (p. 177). I agree with Sullivan in his maintaining this.

Appendix

Kant's Doctrine of Categories: An Attempt at Some Clarification

In this note, I wish to respond to Daya Krishna's note, 'Kant's Doctrine of the Categories: Some Problems' (*JICPR*, Volume XI, Number 3, May–August 1994, pp. 143–44), in which he raises some questions concerning Kant's doctrine of categories as found in his *Critique of Pure Reason*. In doing this, I will not deal with these questions directly, one by one. What I will do is to say a few things, according to my understanding of things, strictly keeping in view these questions. I hope that what I am going to say will help in answering these questions.

(1) Kant mentions twelve categories, which he classifies under four different heads, three under each head: unity, plurality and totality under quantity; reality, negation and limitation under quality; inherence and subsistence (*Substantia et accidents*), causality and dependence (*cause and effect*) and community (reciprocity between agent and patient) under relation; and possibility–impossibility, existence–non–existence and necessity–contingency under modality. Now, I find that all these categories are exactly on a par with one another, in the sense that each one of them is one and not more than one, including those under relation and modality. But they are not on a par with one another, in the sense that they are different from one another under the same head or under different heads. They are

different from one another under the same head, as, for example, there are the different categories of unity, plurality and totality under quantity. They are different from one another under different heads, as for example, the categories under relation, as far as I can see, are relational categories, whereas those under any of the other three heads are not relational categories. Like a relational term in logic, as the terms husband and wife, a relational category may be defined as one which is composed of two terms which are correlative to one another, and that means to say, which are definable only in terms of one another.

I have said above that even the categories under relation are, in each case, one and not more than one. This is now easily seen. I have said above that the categories under relation are relational categories, and I have also defined a relational category. Now, if the categories under relation are relational categories, and a relational category is as I have defined it to be, then it follows that the categories under relation, like relational terms, are in each case, one and not more than one. These categories may be composed of two terms, as indeed they are, but since these two terms are correlative to, or definable only in terms of, one another, these categories, like relational terms, are, in each case, one and not more than one. Now, it only remains for me to show that the categories under relation, as far as I can see, are relational categories. And again, this is easily done as follows: (1) to say that something is a substance (in one sense) is the same thing as to say that it is the support of accidents; and to say that something is an accident is the same thing as to say that it is supported by a substance. (2) To say that something is a cause is the same thing as to say that it is the cause of an effect; and to say that something is an effect is the same thing as to say that it is the effect of a cause. (3) To say that something, say A, is an agent in reciprocity is the same thing as to say that something else, say B, is an agent in reciprocity with A; and to say that B is an agent in reciprocity is the same thing as to say that A is an agent in reciprocity with B. Here following Kant, we can also say that if A and B are agents in reciprocity with one another, then B is a patient in relation to, or is determined by, A, and A is a patient in relation to, or is determined by, B.

I have also said above that the categories under modality are just as well, in each case, one and not more than one. The first category is either the category of possibility or the category of impossibility; and not both. The second category is either the category of existence or the category of non-existence; and not both. The third category is either the category of necessity or the category of non-necessity/contingency; and not both. And all the three categories are either the categories of possibility, existence and necessity, or the categories of impossibility, non-existence; and non-necessity/contingency. It is unthinkable that Kant would have put under one and the same category both possibility and impossibility; under one and the same category both existence and non-existence; and under one and the same category both necessity and non-necessity/contingency.

(2) Kant mentions twelve categories, which he classifies under four different heads. But, as far as I can see, he does not mention whether all the twelve of them, or some number less than that, have to be present in each and every synthesis of the manifold of pure intuitions. The question has been asked whether, according to Kant, all the twelve categories have to be present in each and every synthesis of the manifold of pure intuitions, or only four of them, one category from each head. Now, as Kant himself does not seem to mention anything about it, we have to make up our own mind in this connection. Now, as regards the first alternative in the questions asked; if it is the case, as it may be said to be, that all the three categories under any of the four heads (say, the categories of unity, plurality and totality under the head of quantity) are distinct from one another in such a way that all of them, or even two of them, cannot be present at the same time in the synthesis mentioned; that is to say, not more than one of them can be present at the same time in the synthesis mentioned; then, it follows that all the twelve categories cannot be present in each and every case of the synthesis mentioned, that not more than four of them can

be present in each and every case of the synthesis mentioned, one category from each head.

Further, as regards the second alternative in the question asked above: if, as it appears, according to Kant, every synthesis in the manifold of pure intuitions would be subject to all the four heads of categories (thus, to take a concrete instance, the synthesis of all earthly things as being perishable is subject to the category of unity under the head of quantity, to the category of reality under the head of quality, to the category of substance and accident under the head of relation, and to the category of existence under the category of modality); and if, as we have already seen in the preceding paragraph, not more than four categories can be present in each and every case of the synthesis mentioned, one category from each head; then, it follows that exactly four categories, neither more nor less, would have to be present in each and every case of the synthesis mentioned, one category from each head.

(3) The question has been asked: what is the difference between the categories of reality and negation, which fall under the head of quality, and the categories of existence and non-existence, which fall under the head of modality? I think that the clue to answering this question could be looked for in Kant's table of judgments, upon which his table of categories is claimed to be based. On that basis, we could say the following: the categories of reality and negation, as falling under the head of quality, would in some way relate to the affirmation or denial of something of something, respectively. And the category of existence *or* the category of non-existence, as falling under the head of modality, would in some way relate to the relation of actuality (as distinguished from that of possibility or that of necessity) *or* non-actuality (as distinguished from that of impossibility or that of non-necessity/contingency) of something with another, respectively.

Index